SPEAKING FRANKLY

SPEAKING FRANKLY

What's Wrong with the Democrats and How to Fix It

BARNEY FRANK

TIMES 𝕿 BOOKS

RANDOM HOUSE

Copyright © 1992 by Barney Frank
All rights reserved under International and
Pan-American Copyright Conventions. Published in the
United States by Times Books, a division of Random
House, Inc., New York, and simultaneously in Canada
by Random House of Canada Limited, Toronto.

Library of Congress Cataloging-in-Publication Data
Frank, Barney.
Speaking frankly : what's wrong with the Democrats
and how to fix it / Barney Frank.—1st ed.
        p.   cm.
ISBN 0-812-92010-4
1. Democratic Party (U.S.)   I. Title.
JK2317   1992
324.2736—dc20   91-50134

Manufactured in the United States of America
9 8 7 6 5 4 3 2
FIRST EDITION

TO HERB, AND MY MOTHER

Preface

I HAVE WANTED to write a book for some time, but not so much that I was willing to give up my day job—which means that I have had to do it in the interstices of my work as a Member of Congress. For that reason, it is probably shorter and maybe less elegantly written than it might have been. But I think it is also reflective of the views of many of us who work full time at the job of trying to translate progressive ideas into actual public policy.

It also means that I have more than the usual author's set of debts—to Times Books editor Ken Gellman, who cheerfully competed with my constituents, committee chairs, and journalists for my very finite attention span, to improve the organizational structure of this essay; to friends and supporters who have helped me get here in the first place, and encouraged me to stay through good times and not-so-good ones; to the people who have worked for me, more than I can name after ten years, but a group to whom I am enormously indebted personally, politically and intellectually for all they have done in a joint effort to further our vision of what society ought to look like.

Finally, there is my family. I have been very lucky in a number of ways. None more so than in the character and intellect of my parents, my sisters and brother. To the late Sam Frank, to Ann Lewis, Doris Breay and David Frank, nothing I can say is adequate acknowledgement of all they have done for me.

Two people have been the major influences on my life: my mother, Elsie Frank, who shaped the first couple of decades, and Herb Moses, the man who now shares my life, who has guided me for the last five years. All the really serious mistakes I've made came in that middle period between their spheres of influence.

Contents

SPEAKING FRANKLY

Introduction

IF someone were to write a musical about the Democratic Party of the last generation, it could be called *How to Win Everything in Politics Except the Presidency*. Since 1968 we Democrats have continued to win most elections for Congress, governor, other statewide offices, and the state legislatures. But it is cause for self-congratulation when we break 40 percent in presidential elections.

The unique thing about this twenty-five-year presidential losing streak is that it comes during a time when the issues that divide most Democrats from most Republicans work in our favor. We win the majority of nonpresidential races not by some fluke but because voters on the whole prefer our positions on the specific questions of what government should do about issues such as health care, the environment, the rights of women, social security, housing, and the regulation of the private sector. But when it comes to the presidency, our popular positions on the individual issues do not result in a favorable response from the majority of voters. As William Safire noted in 1968, we Democrats have accomplished a wondrous feat—we have created a whole smaller than the sum of its parts.

How have we managed this? And even more important, how do we stop? This book will try to answer these questions and offer some suggestions for a Democratic agenda that can win at the national level.

It is, as the Marxists used to say when there still were some, no accident that 1968 is the year in which the voters became allergic to Democratic presidents. The sixties were not the party's best decade. During that period we managed to become the targets both of angry groups on the political left who held Democrats responsible for racism and the Vietnam War and of disgusted groups in the center and on the right who blamed us for being far too tolerant of the violent rhetoric and disruptive behavior of the left. The unhappier both groups got with each other, the more they tended to take it out on mainstream liberal Democrats.

We have spent every presidential nominating season since the mid-sixties trying to work our way out of this dilemma. We haven't succeeded. Partially because of the changes Democrats instituted in the presidential nominating process in response to our troubles in 1968, that process offers us the maximum opportunity to remind American voters just what it was that they most disliked about us in the sixties—and this is one opportunity we have rarely passed up.

Our dilemma is and has been how to run a presidential campaign that maximizes our appeal to the broader electorate without so alienating our party's left that its members cause our defeat—by massive abstention; by supporting a third party; by being so disruptive as to make the party look incompetent; or by all of the above.

This is not my personal expression of every politician's secret wish to be all things to all voters. Unfortunately, that's not possible; but much more fortunately, it's not necessary either. The Democrats' task is much more specific and achievable: to win over those voters who, more often than not, vote for Democratic congressmen, governors, and state legislators. This is an identifiable group of voters. They are mostly white— with a growing Hispanic segment—more male than female, working and middle class, and include proportionally more young people than older ones. And, as evidenced by their voting patterns for nonpresidential office, they tend to agree more with the Democrats than with the Republicans on most issues.

These are the swing voters whom we Democrats have alienated by our behavior in seeking the presidency. What has hurt us most has been our obsessive focus on our own internal party concerns and the visible expenditure of so much energy on making sure that the left wing of the party is emotionally secure. My central point is that we can win these swing voters back—enough of them, enough of the time to become competitive for the presidency—without compromising the important principles that differentiate the Democratic and Republican positions on most issues.

To those who say that this cannot be done and should not even be tried lest the party lose its soul, the answer is that this is something virtually all Democratic officeholders do all the time. Remaining true to basic liberal economic and social principles while holding the support of white middle- and working-class males is something congressional and gubernatorial candidates know how to accomplish or they would never win any of these offices in the first place. Because of recent history we will not let ourselves do this at the presidential level (this is the only instance I can think of where self-denial is a legacy of the sixties).

On the one hand, liberal Democrats have suffered from our association with—and occasional defense of—the angry, disruptive protesters of the sixties and seventies and their heirs. These protesters were and are different from any others in recent American history. They were not just critical of specific policies. They were unhappy with America—its politics, its society, and, it seemed, a good many of its people. Those who believed America was a good, decent society wrongly denounced as corrupt by a bunch of misfits and malcontents responded—not with demonstrations but with votes. That is why Democrats have lost five of the last six presidential contests.

On the other hand while Democrats were being blamed by centrist voters for the excesses of the left, we were also under pressure from those on the left who were causing the problems. To them we were, at best, on political probation, and we still are. They have insisted on receiving constant and public reassurance from the Democratic leadership for the last twenty years that we honor their moral commitment, appreciate their unhappiness with America, and remain convinced of the error of having so uncritically supported the status quo in the sixties.

These reassurances have been an important part of the presidential selection process, which on the Democratic side has been skewed heavily on the left, not so much in terms of substance as in rhetoric and symbolism—the sort of things that count for a good deal in presidential races.

The interplay of people and events from the mid-sixties through 1972 has set the tone for Democratic presidential activity in the ensuing twenty years. And a dismal tone it has been.

And this is where Safire's maxim that our whole is smaller than the sum of our parts comes in. Voters do not approach presidential elections by summing up the specific stands of candidates on issues x, y, and z. Elections for the Senate, the House of Representatives, and the state legislatures and governorships are about issues. Elections for the presidency, given its place in our society, turn much more on values. And our problem in essence is that we are so focused as a party on preventing a recurrence of the bitter split between the left and the center that plagued us twenty years ago that we concede the battle of values to the Republicans by letting them portray us as anti-patriotic, skeptical of the work ethic, and soft on crime.

If the unpopular values we have allowed ourselves to be portrayed as supporting were in fact our values, we would be in irreparable political trouble. Fortunately—though frustratingly—they are not. Examination of how Democrats behave when in office show that Democrats in office vote and work for a strong, assertive America; for a workable free-enterprise system; for rewarding those who work hard; and against criminals. But at the presidential level we have allowed ourselves to believe that we shouldn't say all this too loudly, lest we offend the left.

I said above that the important question for the Democrats with regard to the way we lose the presidency is how do we stop. The answer comes from the doctor who was asked by a man holding his arm in an awkward position how to stop the arm from hurting when he did like this. "Easy," said the doctor. "Stop doing like this." For the Democrats, it won't be easy, but we can stop doing like this. We can stop acting as if our most important political problem is keeping our left from feeling betrayed, and focus instead on how to present our commitment to compassionate intervention in the economy, vigorous action on behalf of the environment, fairer taxation, and opposition to discrimination in ways that maximize their appeal to the broader electorate. We can and must do this not out of political expediency but precisely because we care enough about these crusades to want to go beyond advocacy on their behalf to effective action to make them realities.

It is, of course, far easier to advocate this sort of approach than to carry it out. But I believe we have evidence in recent years of how Democrats can press forward vigorously with a genuinely progressive agenda without alienating swing voters the way we have in recent presidential elections. One example, which I discuss later, is the budget dispute between President Bush and congressional Democrats in 1990. By refusing to be goaded by our own left into making a significant tax increase part of the Democratic negotiating posture, and instead forcing President Bush to repudiate his 1988 no-new-tax pledge before we broached the subject, Democrats were able to focus on the question of the fairness of the tax structure, to our governmental and political advantage.

Similarly, we can in my view make major advances governmentally and electorally in the field of international security by contrasting President Bush's insistence on continuing to subsidize our wealthy European and Asian allies with American military largesse to our policy of ending this subsidy and freeing these vast resources for other uses. Taxation and national security are two of the issues President Bush used to great advantage against the Democrats in 1988. I try later in this book to show how both can in fact rebound to our advantage while we remain completely steadfast in our adherence to liberal values.

Finally, I give examples of how I believe we should deal with the other two issues that worked so well for President Bush in 1988, and which are constantly held up as examples of Democratic vulnerability—crime and discrimination, which are closely linked politically.

In what follows I have tried to flesh out the argument I have presented here, to defend it against what I know will be the major objections presented to it, and to give examples of how we liberal Democrats can deal with some of the most difficult issues in ways that are politically and substantively correct in the true sense of that word.

I have not gone into detail in other policy areas—health care, housing, infrastructure, or the environment, for example—because it seems clear to me that these are issues in which the advantage is clearly with us. If I am right that we can present principled positions on taxation, national defense, crime, and discrimination in ways that are either politically advantageous or at worst politically neutral, our advantages in these other areas will help reestablish our hold on the presidency, and if I'm wrong about these four, I personally plan on learning how to live in opposition for the next twenty years.

I know that after reading this some people on the left are already bristling, suspicious that this is the prelude to my advocating a wholesale abandonment of liberal positions on pseudopragmatic grounds. It isn't and I don't. I will argue later for some changes in what liberals stand for, and even more in how we present our platform; much of that argument is rooted in my views on how we can enhance our electoral appeal. In some cases my own policy preferences coincide with my view of what makes the most electoral sense, and when they do, I will say so. What I will not do is be dissuaded from proposing some politically motivated changes in Democratic positions by the charge that experience assures me will be forthcoming: that I secretly oppose these positions, or else I would have confidence that with enough skillful work, we could convert the voters to our way of thinking.

Nor am I prepared to acknowledge a lack of political courage, moral fiber, or deep commitment because I am prepared to take the electorate's views into account in thinking about how the Democrats can win the presidency. It is precisely because politicians should be serious about affecting society for the better that we are obligated to consider what strategy is likeliest to succeed. This is definitely not to say that Democrats should let vote counts displace commitment in deciding our platform. It is to insist that we must recognize that electoral calculations are a morally relevant constraint on our principles if we are serious about implementing them. Deciding just when and how to blend ideological and pragmatic considerations is the central and very difficult task Democrats face. We do not have even a chance of doing it satisfactorily until we explicitly reject both those who ignore the need for it and those who denounce the effort as inherently morally flawed.

What's Wrong?

DEMOCRATS usually win when the voters are focusing on issues, and Republicans almost always win when voters are concerned with values.

Democratic positions on the issues—the concrete questions of what government policy ought to be in the areas of health care, the environment, the needs of the elderly, housing, transportation, education—have generally had greater appeal to voters than the alternatives supported by Republicans. But when the difference between the parties is on what basic values they stand for in the public's mind—values such as patriotism, hard work, respect for the law and for the rights and property of others—the Republicans win the debate.

This explains why Democrats have been consistently successful in congressional, gubernatorial, and state legislative elections—contests that regularly turn on what government ought to do in specific cases. And it is why Republicans win the presidency: in presidential elections Americans are voting their overall view of what basic values American society ought to embrace.

The battle of issues versus values thus explains why Ronald Reagan won one of the greatest electoral triumphs in our history in 1984 despite the fact that a majority of voters disagreed with him on so many specific issues. Not only did Reagan succeed in embodying those values that most Americans want to see as the basis for our national life; with significant cooperation from the Democrats themselves he managed to give the impression that we were on the wrong side of some core American values, and only tepidly in favor of others.

That voters apply different criterion to different elections is one of those basic facts that seem to be better understood by some of politics' least cerebral practitioners than by some of its most thoughtful analysts. Politicians are often much less surprised than pundits when, for example, a person who regularly tops the ticket for city council fails dismally when running for some executive office. And the most important example of this in American politics is the presidency. Voters look on that office differently—more respectfully, less parochially, as the office where America must show its best face to the world. Nowhere else in our system are the people as likely to "vote up"—to cast their ballots not so much to represent themselves and their interests as to embody their favored vision of the nation as a whole.

Two examples from the 1988 and 1990 elections illustrate this essential political point. The first is George Bush and the textile quota bill; the second is the American flag. A sine qua non for election to Congress from the Carolinas is strong support for legislation that limits imports of textile and textile products. Liberals and conservatives, Democrats and Republicans from these two states regularly put aside all of their differences to form a united bloc behind this bill, which is why it has twice passed the Congress. Unfortunately for its proponents, however, the bills were vetoed each time—once by Ronald Reagan, with George Bush's support, and the second time, after he was elected, of course, by Bush himself.

Bush entered the North and South Carolina presidential primaries in 1988 as a man who had not only backed the veto of a bill very popular with Carolina voters but who had made clear his intention to veto the bill again if it came before him as president. His chief opponent was Robert Dole, the Republican Senate leader who had a very different record on this issue. Dole had broken with President Reagan to help push this important bill through. But Bush's opposition to the textile bill did not hurt him in either the primaries or the general election. He easily carried each state both times. What voters in these states would never have tolerated in a senator or representative had no discernible effect on their decision about who should be president.

Very much the reverse is true regarding the question of the American flag. In 1988 George Bush gained heavily at the expense of Michael Dukakis by hammering away at Dukakis's veto of a Massachusetts bill that required teachers to lead their students in the Pledge of Allegiance. As many noted at the time, Bush's use of this matter clearly contributed to his portrayal of Dukakis as someone who lacked sympathy with the basic values of most Americans. But Republicans failed to use the flag to similar advantage in the 1990 congressional races. They had threatened to target Democrats who had opposed the constitutional amendment to ban flag burning, but their efforts proved unsuccessful. Of the 165 Democrats in the House and Senate who opposed that amendment in 1990 and ran for reelection, only four lost, and no one has argued that the flag vote was of any significance in any of these defeats.

Electoral outcomes turn on many factors, and single explanations are almost never adequate to explain complex results. But these examples illustrate how issues dominate elections for lower offices while values play a major role at the presidential level. The question of what the level of textile imports should be is a quintessential issue: the answer the government gives to this question will have concrete effects on people's lives. Voters care much more about the effects of that legislation than they do about the symbolic values the decision may express—and they expect their congressional representatives to protect their interests. Pledging allegiance to the flag, or preventing others from burning it, involves symbolic values. A politician's stand on them does not directly affect the course of voters' daily lives, but it tells the voters something about what that candidate thinks is morally important.

For most of the last twenty-five years, it has been on questions of values that we encounter our most serious political problems. Democrats have come to be perceived as insufficiently pro-American, both internationally and at home; unenthusiastic about free enterprise, especially the principle that one should work for one's keep; unwilling and unprepared to move harshly against criminals; and disrespectful of the way average Americans live their lives.

I disagree with most of this indictment of the Democrats. The accusation that we have been careless of national security, unsympathetic to free enterprise, soft on crime, or disrespectful of average Americans is flatly wrong.

The record of Democrats in office—members of the U.S. Senate and House, governors, state legislators, attorneys general, etc.—bears little relation to the caricature of the self-hating American bent on forcing the middle class to carry the undeserving poor on its back, and unwilling to protect honest citizens against criminals. For forty-five years Democrats in Congress have carried forward their commitment to a policy of massive military expenditures to deter Communist advances. The major debates have been about how to spend 5 percent or less of military budgets, and there has also been complete Democratic support for such efforts as the massive—and successful—program of military aid to the Afghan rebels.

Democratic district attorneys, attorneys general, and mayors have worked vigorously to enforce the criminal laws, and no objective look at the welfare payment level in states controlled by Democrats could conclude that we have erred on the side of excessive generosity.

This does not mean that there are no differences between the parties. Indeed, the divisions between Democrats and Republicans on issues today are clearer than they have been for more than fifty years. In America today, if you want to predict what an unknown public official will do on a wide range of issues, and you are allowed to ask only one question about him or her, you will in the great majority of cases get more guidance by asking the official's partisan affiliation than any other fact. This is especially true now that the growth of African American voter participation and national economic trends have made the South much less different from the rest of America. Thus, *Congressional Quarterly*'s Conservative Coalition Index, which shows how often a majority of southern Democrats in the House of Representatives vote with a majority of

Republicans and against a majority of other Democrats shows a dramatic drop over the last twenty years. In the years 1969 through 1972, southern Democrats joined Republicans against nonsouthern Democrats on 26.5 percent of all House roll calls. By the period from 1987 through 1990, this had dropped by almost two-thirds to 9.75 percent.) The point is that these differences, while fairly clear-cut, occur within the broad framework of values shared by nearly all Americans.

Within the framework of a market economy, Democrats have supported far more government intervention to protect the environment, greater efforts toward some redistribution of income, and more active regulation of private enterprise on behalf of workers and consumers. Republicans have argued that too much activity on any of these fronts would damage the ability of the free-enterprise system to produce the greatest amount of goods and services. On foreign affairs there is broad agreement of both goals and methods, but the Republicans have been more supportive of American military action while the Democrats have argued for a stronger emphasis on defending America's economic interests. During the eighties the two parties on the national level have been for approximately the same level of federal spending, with the Republicans preferring higher military numbers and lower domestic totals than the Democrats.

I should acknowledge that I am making a conscious choice here to define the Republican and Democratic parties ideologically by cumulating what their respective officeholders do in practice. Theoretically, one could argue that what a party stands for is best defined by its platform or what polls show to be the views of those who consider themselves party members. But in America, with federalism and the decentralization of power, knowing any or all of these things would be of little predictive value concerning the relation between that party's success and how it will govern. For those who judge a party by the effect its political success has on public policy, the record of its officeholders is the most relevant criterion.

For Democrats the critical question then becomes why a critical bloc of voters refuses to use this criterion in presidential elections and why they regularly reject our presidential candidates even while voting for Democrats for most other offices. The answer is that in recent elections Democrats have consistently put our worst foot forward in the presidential nominating process.

Here, Democrats give the appearance that we are further to the left on fundamentals than is actually the case and that we are more afraid of angering our own left than of losing the votes of the undecided voters in the middle.

Mainstream liberal Democrats have been intimidated by the left politically to some degree, but morally to an even greater extent. And, because they are intimidated, the bulk of liberal Democrats cannot enthusiastically embrace the political strategy of reconciling a liberal agenda with mainstream values in the way that offers us the best chance to win elections and carry out Democratic public policies.

In presidential years liberal Democrats must not allow the left to insist that our nominee spend most of the primary season and a good part of the election campaign reassuring the left of his or her ideological reliability. Instead, we should let our candidates focus on presenting a Democratic agenda in a way that is most likely to appeal to a majority of the voters. This does not mean turning our backs on the poor, or abandoning opposition to various forms of bias or softening our insistence on a much cleaner environment and a much smaller military budget. It does mean that our most important challenge in the 1992 campaign and in future presidential elections is to make clear that Democratic positions are fully consistent with the values of patriotism, free enterprise, working hard for one's self and one's family, and holding people to a standard of behavior fully respectful of the person and property of others. The experience of Michael Dukakis in 1988 illustrates our problem—an electorate that is predisposed to believe that liberals are deficient in their commitment to basic American values. As E. J. Dionne notes in his excellent analysis of that campaign, ''Bush . . . took Michael Dukakis—who is about as much of a hippie as Abbie Hoffman was a Marine—and cast him as the representative of everything that went wrong in the 60's.''

Why was the public so ready to accept this caricature? It was not simply that Dukakis had vetoed a bill calling for compulsory flag salutes and presided over a system that furloughed Willie Horton. After twenty years of watching the Democratic nominating process, swing voters were ready to believe not that Dukakis's actions were motivated by some generally acceptable principles that had been misapplied in the case of Horton and misunderstood in the case of the pledge, but that as a mainstream liberal Dukakis really wasn't strongly against criminals nor was he very patriotic. Dukakis did not, it is true, fight back against these attacks as soon as he should have, but even if he had done so earlier, he would have faced a serious problem because of the predisposition of swing voters to believe the worst of Democratic candidates on these issues.

The Legacy of the 1960s

The reason these kinds of tactics work against Democrats in national elections has its genesis in the most agonizing period in American political history for liberals—the mid and late sixties—with its traumas of racial disturbances and the Vietnam War.

The emotionally wracking disputes over these issues, and the unusually bitter intraparty fighting that ensued, shaped the Democratic presidential nominating processes in 1968 and 1972 and have left a deep imprint on our party. The two most important political handicaps under which the Democratic Party still labors grow out of these events and the various reactions to them.

First, it was during this period that significant numbers of middle- and working-class whites began to regard the national Democrats as having a flawed set of values and became increasingly alienated from elements within the party. One of the unusual characteristics of the politics of the mid-sixties and early seventies is the ferocity of the dissent that existed. The racial turmoil and the fight over Vietnam brought a degree of bitterness and disruption to our politics rarely seen since the Civil War.

But the disagreement and anger were not limited to specific policies. Many of the dissenters were convinced that America's actions toward its racial minorities and its conduct in Indochina were not only wrong but immoral; and these immoral policies were not isolated errors, but the logical result of the rottenness of American society. Many protesters were determined either to remake society radically or at least to make it pay the price for its rottenness. Some who did not fully agree with this denunciation of America and the disruptive protest it spawned nonetheless supported the militant protesters because they shared much of their emotional revulsion at the objectionable policies.

Unfortunately, the people who paid the price were not the conservatives who most strongly opposed the dissenters. It was liberal Democrats who bore—and more to the point, still bear—the brunt of the electoral consequences. Those who were causing the social disruption—from rioting in cities to shutting down college campuses—were seen by Middle Americans to be elements of the Democratic coalition. The anger many Americans felt at being denounced so harshly and having their lives interfered with was directed not just at those who did the denouncing and disrupting; but at those with whom they were seen to be politically affiliated—the liberal Democrats.

Liberal Democrats exacerbated the situation by failing to disassociate themselves from the dissenters. What many Americans saw during that period was a Democratic Party that sought not only to justify the actions of looters, arsonists, draft dodgers, and social misfits but to conciliate them and to reward their misbehavior by accommodating their demands. In contrast, they saw a Republican Party that defended American values against unfair attacks and sought to enforce reasonable standards of public behavior. For some voters who had previously considered themselves to be part of a Democratic coalition, defending the interests of average people against the wealthy Republicans, the Democrats were beginning to appear instead as defenders of the hostile and somewhat alien Them.

The second handicap liberals carry from the sixties is a reluctance to engage those on our left in political battle—and it is an even greater handicap because the reluctance is wholly unrequited. Making liberals the main political victims of radical dissent was very much what the radicals intended. (What they did not intend were the ultimate long-term consequences of this liberal-bashing.)

The eagerness of the left to discredit mainstream liberals and the unwillingness of those liberals to fight back effectively resulted from the same cause: the disputes over both racial politics and the war in Vietnam that began as disagreements within the liberal wing of the Democratic Party. Many of the most disaffected on the party's left blamed what they saw as the immoral policies not on conservatives, or even moderate Republicans, but on liberal Democrats. It was Democratic mayors and their political allies in virtually every big city who were the targets of the furious indignation of blacks and their ideological supporters. Indeed, one of the few mayors to avoid the rioters' wrath was the Republican John Lindsay in New York.

In the case of the war, the issue was even clearer. For many liberals, the villains were Lyndon Johnson, a Democrat, who was carrying out policies begun by John Kennedy, another Democrat, with the support of a Democratic Congress. It was Hubert Humphrey, the leading liberal Democrat of the late fifties and early sixties who carried the banner for the prowar forces in the pivotal 1968 Democratic presidential nominating process. And, in case there were any dissenting Democrats who were insufficiently enraged at liberals over racial and/or war policies, Humphrey's nomination by the "old rules" in the midst of new turmoil took care of that.

For mainstream liberals then, 1968 provided the worst of both worlds. On the right they were held responsible for disruption, dissent, and the emergence of anti-Americanism as a political force in America. On the left those very dissenters and disrupters were so outraged by the continuation of the war, Humphrey's nomination and, after the convention, by the brutal misbehavior of the Chicago police, that they contributed in various ways and with varying degrees of enthusiasm to the election of Richard Nixon.

While the left got angrier, the liberal targets of their anger were conflicted. Morally, liberal Democratic officeholders felt a great deal of sympathy with those objecting to racial conditions in America's cities, even as they were being held responsible for perpetuating them. Similarly, liberals began to doubt the rightness of America's cause in Vietnam as the years progressed. The overreaction by law enforcement authorities to various forms of protest added significantly to liberal ambivalence about opposing the protesters.

Politically, while liberal Democratic leaders worried about erosion on their right, they simultaneously had to be concerned about the sort of defections from the left that had contributed to Humphrey's defeat. As a result of both of these factors, even those liberal leaders who disagreed sharply with the strategy and tactics of those on the party's left were reluctant to say so, and when they did voice disagreement, too often they did so apologetically. This usually succeeded in further annoying the left without reassuring those in the middle.

The events of the late 1960s established three patterns of political behavior among Democrats which, in the 1980s, resulted in our presidential candidates being viewed unfavorably by many voters who continued to support Democratic positions on basic government issues.

First, the controversies of 1968 left a large number of Democrats intellectually and emotionally fixated on the Democratic presidential nominating process as the key political event; actually winning the presidential election became a matter of secondary interest. Second, for the left in the Democratic Party, this all-important nominating process became a continuing fight for the party's soul, in which all contestants would be required to make frequent, uncompromising, and deeply felt affirmations of commitment to post-1968 progressive values. Third, those liberal and moderate Democrats who increasingly came to view the influence of the left as detrimental to the Democrats' chances of presidential victory refrained from saying so very loudly, lest they reignite the kind of gut-wrenching, intraparty fights that caused so much grief in 1968.

All three of these factors were strengthened initially by the false comfort Democrats derived from the narrow margin of Humphrey's defeat. If, with all of the problems plaguing him, Humphrey could still come within a hair of winning, then the Democrats' problem could be seen more as one of getting our own house in order than of gearing up to fight growing conservative strength. And that is exactly what Democrats set out to do. In the period after 1968 many in the party focused on completely democratizing the presidential nominating process, so as to avoid a repeat of that year.

To the pragmatic liberals—the people who had previously had the most influence in presidential nominations—this was a way to ensure that the nominee led a reasonably united party into the fall elections. For them the ideal scenario for 1972 was for the party to choose as its nominee a mainstream liberal like Senator Edmund Muskie, after a spirited, open but ultimately friendly nominating process. Instead, of course, George McGovern swept Muskie aside by appealing to the deep strains of dissatisfaction with the status quo that had taken root in the late sixties. McGovern then learned painfully that these strains went far deeper within the Democratic Party than they did in the nation as a whole. The very themes which McGovern used so successfully against Muskie—identification with elements of the counterculture—came back to help overwhelm him in November. But what should have been a clear lesson went largely unlearned. For a sufficiently large number of Democrats the lesson of 1972 was the opportunity that the wide-open nominating process offered for enforcing ideological orthodoxy.

For the next sixteen years, taking advantage of those opportunities continued to be the dominant motive for far too many Democrats. The very openness of the nomination process made presidential nominating activity the major form of grass-roots activity for Democrats. By 1974 we were spending about twenty months each presidential season debating each other and only three months fighting with the Republicans.

The details of the nomination contests of 1972 through 1988 are not relevant here; but an analysis of these races shows that party activists paid very little attention to which candidate could best win in November and a good deal of attention to making sure that all candidates reassured an ever-suspicious Democratic left of their bona fides.

In presidential politics, the Democratic left should learn something from the Republican right about how to share in real power.* The internal battles in George

*As of December 1991, it seemed as if the reverse might be happening, with elements of the Republican right led by Pat Buchanan adopting a much more demanding—and potentially damaging—form of intraparty politics.

Bush's party have also been fierce on some issues. The ideological gap between the Republican far right and the Republican center is greater than the one that separates Democratic liberals from the party's ideological left. But when it comes time to pick a presidential candidate, the Republican right does not insist that the rest of the party spend all its political resources and emotional energy to keep them happy. Compare the behavior of Pat Robertson, the standard bearer of the Republican right, and Jesse Jackson, the Democrat farthest to the left, in 1988. Both were defeated in the primaries, but by the time of the convention Robertson had become an enthusiastic and helpful supporter of George Bush. Jackson, though he supported Dukakis during the campaign, made the Democrats court him publicly in a way that reenforced the perception that Democrats care more about pacifying their left than about winning over the center.

The Tyranny of the Notsapostas

Not only has the left loudly pressured Democratic nominees into constant courtship, our ideological militants have also limited the Democrats' ability to defend themselves from the Republicans.

In the last twenty-four years Democrats have been the targets of steady attacks from the right—attacks on their patriotism, moral strength, and commitment to American ideals. Yet Democratic presidential candidates have been reluctant to respond to these attacks; instead of joining the battle, they've declared themselves above the fight. This is the approach Michael Dukakis took in his race against George Bush. "I won't give into that garbage," he seemed to say. "I won't let them have the satisfaction of getting to me."

But Bush was getting to Dukakis where it counted— with the voters—in the way that Republicans have gotten to Democratic presidential candidates for twenty-five years. And the time has come to recognize that trying to ignore this line of attack is a fatal political error. All too often liberals have responded as Dukakis did to these sorts of attacks, by ignoring the specifics of the charges on the grounds that "these are not the real issues."

This can work at the congressional, senatorial, and gubernatorial level, especially if the candidate is well enough known so that voters find it unlikely that he has a secret fondness for serial killers or a desire to expropriate single-family homeowners. It does not work well at the presidential level when the candidate is far less familiar, and particularly when he is a Democrat suffering from the voters' negative view of his party's general approach.

Given the history of the last twenty-five years, we cannot simply "rise above" these distortions; we have to refute them. Unfortunately, what has prevented this has been the notsaposta, a political phenomenon of the right as well as the left. A notsaposta is a truth that members of a political party are told by ideologues that they cannot acknowledge, lest they give aid and comfort to their enemy. For Democrats the most important notsaposta issues have been crime and foreign policy.

If you are a liberal officeholder, many of your hardest-working supporters will tell you that you are "notsaposta" denounce the viciousness of those who commit violent crimes because your statements might be used by others to argue for the death penalty or could contribute, indirectly, to racial stereotyping. Until very recently many on the left argued that we were notsaposta point out that the American government was morally superior to the Soviet government by every relevant criterion or that America's role in the world has been a positive one over the last forty-five years. The risk was that such sentiments could be used by Republicans to justify more military spending and foreign interventions. Variations of these arguments are now used to discourage liberals from noting that George Bush is morally superior to a variety of third-world dictators, or that America today continues to be one of the places in the world where political and artistic expression is the freest.

In practice, then, the notsaposta is the passionately sincere but grievously mistaken view that acknowledging a troubling truth will weaken a party's ability to resist the conclusions that its political opponents might draw from those truths. What happens, in fact, is almost always exactly the opposite. The failure to join your political enemies in affirming some beliefs that are strongly and widely held by voters weakens your ability to win them over to your side because you effectively concede these issues to your opponents. The Democrats' silence makes us suspect.

Clinging to the notsaposta mind-set has particularly hurt our party in the debate over how to respond to violent crime. There is nothing that liberal politicians are told we are notsaposta say more than that people who commit violent crimes against others are bad and should be punished. It is not that our left wing approves of muggers, rapists, and murderers. But they fear that if we harshly condemn criminals on moral grounds or if we sympathize too deeply with their victims, we will contribute to a climate in which the rights to fair trials are undermined and punishments will become harsh to the point of counterproductivity.

But precisely because liberals have restrained themselves from criticizing criminals, we have been severely handicapped when debating the issue. First, accusations like those George Bush leveled against Michael Dukakis in 1988 resonate with the voters far beyond what the facts could begin to justify. It makes sense to many voters that a Democratic governor would support a furlough program for murderers—out of a concern for murderer's rights. Second, conservatives dictate the terms of the debate on criminal justice issues more than they would if we equaled them in the vehemence of our denunciation of people who rob, assault, and kill others. If one side in a debate accompanies its proposals with scathing attacks on criminals while the other side tones down its criticism and stresses the need to understand the social conditions that underlie the crime, those voters who deeply resent muggers and thieves will respond predictably.

Similarly, in foreign policy, arguments for reduced Pentagon spending are likely to lose if they seem to be based on disapproval of America's international involvements. Those who support higher military budgets can then couch their argument as the pro-American thing to do. No one understood or acted on this political phenomenon more skillfully than Ronald Reagan. Because he embraced and passionately articulated the values of thrift, free enterprise, law and order, and patriotism—which liberals avoided in obedience to the notsapostas—Reagan managed to turn the debate between him and the Democrats into a debate on basic American values, with the Democrats on the wrong side. We tried to beat Reagan solely on the issues because we were notsaposta compete with him in proclaiming our allegiance to the important values underlying them. So to the swing voters in 1980, 1984, and later in 1988, our silence became a sign that the Republicans were right in doubting Democrats' attachment to our country, its free-market economy, and its citizens' right to be free from crime.

And this frustrating situation continues. In the Democratic Party today many of the most principled liberals who hold elective office understand that we suffer from our failure to express what we believe in rhetoric that will appeal to swing voters. But they are reluctant to act on this conviction. Most of us believe deeply in mainstream American values and the positions we take are wholly consistent with these principles. Yet we fail to convey these beliefs in our speeches or support them in our party conventions because we fear angering those Democrats on the left who believe it is inappropriate for us to speak out in this manner.

Thus, our major task at the presidential level is not to engage in a radical overhaul of the basic Democratic principles of public policy. As I will argue later, the evidence is clear that these positions are more popular than not with a majority of voters. Instead, we must recognize that we have done a poor job of putting these policy views in the proper context in presidential elections—that we have focused so much of our energies on not offending the left that we have had too little remaining to win over the center.

Some policy changes are in order, especially in the area of crime, where we should show more enthusiasm for the need for effective law enforcement, and in the regulatory area, where we should decrease our enthusiasm for telling people how to make choices about their own health and well-being—such as insisting on keeping the fifty-five-mile-per-hour speed limit everywhere. And there are issues where what is needed is for liberals to understand the importance of prudence, where a core liberal position may be so unpopular in either a region or the whole country as to make it a poor candidate for litmus-test status. Gun control and the death penalty are relevant here.

The debate over the civil rights bill in Congress in 1990 and 1991 is an excellent example both of what we need to do and the problems we encounter in trying to do it. While it is a congressional issue rather than part of a presidential campaign, it illustrates both our vulnerability to unfair attacks from the right and the resistance we encounter on our left when we try to defuse these attacks.

Democrats began in 1990 with a civil rights bill that was drafted to overturn several Supreme Court decisions that limited antidiscrimination remedies, but in a manner that clearly avoided the accusation that it would mandate quotas. President Bush and his allies on the right denounced it as a quota bill notwithstanding this, and the House failed to override his veto in 1990.

In 1991 the Democrats came back with a bill explicitly banning quotas, and containing other provisions aimed at softening the bill's edges enough to win over the necessary votes to override a second presidential veto. During much of the debate in early 1991, two things resulted. Despite the bill's provisions to the contrary, the president continued to claim it required quotas, and convinced many voters that he was correct. This was not because of what was in the bill so much as because these voters were predisposed to believe that mandating quotas was just what the Democrats would do if their minority and feminist allies demanded it.

At the same time, frustratingly, many representatives of the latter groups, especially feminists, bitterly denounced the Democratic congressional leadership for making any concessions at all. The unrefuted fact that a bill lacking these compromises could not become law, and the fact that the bill as presented still went a very long way toward combating discrimination counted for very little with these critics. And characteristically the great majority of Democrats who knew that such flexibility was not only necessary but morally the most desirable course for accomplishing the civil rights movement's goals held back from answering their critics on the left, leaving the impression that there was no principled answer to the criticisms. Thus, we had, as far as the public was concerned, the worst of both worlds. Voters in the center and on the right found us guilty of quota-mongering, while those on the left thought we had sold out their principles. For mainstream liberals both criticisms were as wrong substantively as they were damaging politically.

Substantively, the liberal position was vindicated in late October of 1991 when the president agreed to the bill he had essentially been denouncing. The president felt pressured by the ire of many women at the abusive treatment Anita Hill received during the confirmation hearings of Supreme Court Associate Justice Clarence Thomas as well as the success of Klansman David Duke in the Louisiana gubernatorial runoff. Politically, however, liberals got much less credit for the passage of the bill than we deserved. Some on the left continued, with little justification, to criticize congressional liberals for selling out while Bush continued—with absolutely no justification—to claim that he had saved America from quotas.

The left's criticism of the mainstream liberal position on the civil rights bill is not of course an isolated instance. It is emblematic of a deep and powerful political current within the Democratic Party, which gives a prescription for victory very different from the one I am advocating. This is the view that what we Democrats need is the courage of our convictions—the willingness to articulate a firm, uncompromising liberalism that will bring us victory without having to accommodate ourselves to those on our right.

Neither to the Left nor to the Right

There are some liberals who argue that a gap in our political system rather than voters' ambivalence about liberalism accounts for the divided electoral pattern of the last twenty-five years.

They contend that there is a national majority prepared to support presidential candidates who stand forthrightly for liberal principles but that the Democrats have failed to nominate standard-bearers who could tap into this sentiment. If Democrats nominate someone who will argue in compelling terms for universal health care, minority rights, progressive tax increases, tough policies against polluters, social justice as our main bulwark against crime, and a kinder, gentler America overseas, these people say, the voters will respond favorably.

Among those who advocate this position, there is a difference in emphasis between those who stress the need for Democrats to expand the electorate and those who concentrate more on persuading current voters to change their voting patterns. Like much in our politics, there is a racial aspect to this distinction. People who talk of Democrats winning by increasing the total turnout usually focus on the African-American and Hispanic populations. Those who say that a forthright progressivism will capture votes more often have in mind winning white voters back to the Democratic side. Logically, these two positions are fully consistent. But in practice reconciling the two is trickier than the proponents of either version generally admit.

Yet the differences between the two sides of this

coin are part of a larger problem with the whole strategy of winning by moving to our left. As articulated by its most ardent advocates, it won't work. I say this with greater reluctance than I say anything else in this essay. I would be delighted if we could reverse our presidential losing streak in this manner. A strategy that aims to burnish our appeal on the left would be ideologically pleasing to most party activists and, in part for that reason, would be relatively easy to implement. But if the problem were this easily solved, it would almost certainly not have existed in the first place.

The insistence that Democratic presidential candidates continually reassure liberals of their purity is a major cause for the decline of our appeal to the swing voters.

And the reaction of the swing voters is not the only problem with this strategy. In neither of its variants are there political facts to back up its claims. First, consider the argument that bringing millions of new, previously unregistered voters into the political process will ensure victory for the Democrats. It is true that there are tens of millions of people who do not vote in presidential elections. But changing this behavior is more difficult and less clearly a pro-Democratic enterprise than many might think. Potential Democrats among those who don't vote are especially numerous among members of racial minorities, and it is of course true that Democratic candidates do better as more African-American, Puerto Rican, or Mexican-Americans vote. But the reasons voter turnout is lower among these groups than among society as a whole have much less to do with dissatisfaction with political choices than with poverty, social disorganization, and a deep alienation from society. Getting more people in the lowest socioeconomic categories to vote is an extraordinarily difficult task, unlikely to be achieved by sharpening the rhetorical bite of Democratic candidates.

The other major demographic category with relatively low voter turnout is that of younger voters. Getting those under thirty to vote more regularly might be easier, but it is by no means clear that this would help Democrats. For a variety of reasons younger voters have been less Democratic, not more, in their inclinations.

Recent public-opinion polls, in fact, lead to the conclusion that higher turnout would have made no significant difference in the outcome of the last three presidential elections. The conclusion to be drawn from comparing presidential and nonpresidential outcomes is similarly unhelpful to this argument. Democrats do better in nonpresidential contests, which usually generate low turnout.

Neither is there statistical support for this proposition in comparing turnout figures in different nonpresidential elections. I know of no evidence that voter turnout is significantly higher in elections in which the Democratic candidates are outspokenly on the left as opposed to those with more moderate Democratic candidates. It is true that the presence of a black or Hispanic candidate in a close race increases turnout among the particular group represented, but that is a different phenomenon, and it is not transferable to candidates who offer ideological sympathy without racial identification.

We have had a very good test recently of the hypothesis that the right kind of candidate can enhance Democratic chances by bringing large numbers of previously alienated voters into the process—the candidacies of Jesse Jackson. To some extent in 1984, and without question in 1988, Jesse Jackson was the sort of candidate this argument calls for. He was—and is—passionately, eloquently commited to a strongly liberal agenda and he campaigned explicitly on the premise that he would win in part by broadening the electorate. He didn't. There was some increased turnout among black voters in primaries, but this falls short of proving the point at issue here on three related grounds: (1) the increased participation was almost exclusively among black voters, even though Jackson's message was aimed at energizing the poor of all races; (2) because of the limited scope of his ability to bring out additional voters, Jackson did not succeed in bringing out nearly as many new voters as this theory would predict; and (3) because of this he did not win the nomination. And if the argument is raised that this is not a good test because Jackson lost a nomination, not the general election, that only strengthens the rebuttal: if a candidate cannot win the Democratic nomination by broadening the participation rate with appeals to the left, he can hardly expect greater success in November with an electorate that is both more conservative than the primary electorate and also contains to begin with a significantly larger percentage of the voters. Jesse Jackson was not, of course, the perfect candidate. But then no one is. And no one I can think of could have filled the role of tribune of populist causes as well as he did in the 1988 primary season. If Jesse Jackson's performance in that year could not bring out millions of additional voters—in hotly contested primaries that were receiving great amounts of media coverage—I am skeptical that anyone else would do better.

And the unpleasant fact that Democrats must face up to is that while Jackson did turn out some new voters, he also succeeded in turning off many others. Part of this has to do with Jackson's race. But the bulk of the negative effect Jackson had on Democratic chances in November was the result of his rhetoric. This is at the heart of the dilemma, especially for those who believe that the Democrats' path to victory is a straightforward march to the left.

This brings us to the second variant of that argument: the view that we will win back the swing voters—those who vote Democratic for everything but the presidency—only by an uncompromising reaffirmation of basic liberal principles. There is a great deal in this argument with which I agree. Properly presented, traditional Democratic economic themes—such as those at issue in the 1990 budget fight—have considerable popular appeal. Strong evidence for this proposition can be drawn from 1988, when Michael Dukakis made the only gains he scored in the postnomination period by campaigning as an economic liberal in fact, if not by name. But it is far from the relatively uncomplicated route to victory that its advocates represent.

Witness, again, the Jackson campaign. The rhetoric Jackson employed to persuade the previously nonvoting of his sympathy with them unfortunately persuaded many of those already voting of his antipathy to their interests. Some of this may be attributable to Jackson himself. But it was also the consequence of an inherent tension between the two aspects of the "go to the left" strategy. Those who seek to motivate the alienated to abandon their state of self-disenfranchisement tend to do so by expressing complete sympathy for their plight. "We understand your bitterness at a system which has abandoned you," the nonvoters are told, "and we need you to join us so that we can radically rearrange it in ways that will benefit you." The temptation seems irresistible for those pursuing this course to go beyond specific programmatic promises and base their approach on a critique of racism, economic inequality, and insensitivity in American society.

Telling those who have done least well in our society that the problem is the racism and economic unfairness of the system may well be the best way to appeal to them. It is the worst possible message to send to the swing voters who have been pivotal in deciding presidential races.

Unfortunately, it is a message too many Democrats are unable to resist sending, even when their focus is not on bringing in the nonparticipants but simply in winning back the swing voters. And the prevalence of this tendency, in turn, is why simply stressing popular liberal issues is a strategy more easily asserted than executed.

Theoretically, it is possible to construct a campaign that focuses on the need for tougher environmental rules, universal health insurance, the right of women to choose abortions, more spending on education and public transportation, and a diversion of funds from American military spending in Europe and Japan into domestic needs. Practically, the emotional and intellectual tenor of many Democratic activists makes it hard for them to resist the tendency to generalize these specific proposals for improvements in our society into a generalized criticism of its shortcomings. This is where we begin to lose votes—where we cross the line from debate on the issues, where we do well, to an atmosphere in which we seem to be denigrating basic values to which a majority of voters subscribe.

Even those who do not themselves cross that line in campaigning on popular progressive issues will be at a disadvantage as long as other Democrats do. There is nothing unfair about this—individual citizens have a right to object to guilt by association, but that defense will probably not work when invoked by members of a party about a widespread party practice. Thus, the view that Democrats can win the presidency by a sharper, clearer liberalism is lacking not because it is inaccurate but because it is sometimes misleading and usually incomplete.

The misleading aspect is that it overestimates liberalism's appeal and underestimates the baggage it has acquired. When people say that the way to win is to reemphasize basic liberal goals, they tend to act as if from the electoral standpoint, the more liberalism the better. Thus, we get speeches that go beyond advocacy of universal health insurance coverage to scathing denunciations of America's unique moral shortcomings as one of the few industrial nations not to provide such benefits.

Swing voters can be won over by a proper description of the liberal program goals that respond to their needs. But they are more likely to be repelled than attracted by a total package that explains the need for these programmatic changes by a graphic explanation of America's societal weaknesses. This is how the popular parts get accumulated into an unpopular whole.

True, not all of those who stress the programmatic strengths of liberalism make the mistake of wrapping their package in the wrong set of values. But so many voters have come to identify Democratic presidential politics with the values they dislike that silence on the subject is not enough.

The notion that all will be well if we simply speak clearly enough about liberal programmatic goals does not cause this problem. But it induces exactly the opposite mind-set in our candidates from that needed to resolve it.

One last point must be added to this discussion. There are, as we have noted, large numbers of Democrats who continue to win office at every level below the presidency. If stressing solid liberal values as forcefully and uncompromisingly as possible was such an obvious formula for victory, it would presumably be one not only advocated but followed by Democratic governors, senators, House members, attorneys general, and state legislators.

There are, of course, many in these categories who do win in this fashion. But there are also large numbers who take other tactical paths—I doubt that anyone has any idea which approach has more adherents, or even how many variations there are on the themes. But one thing is very clear: among those in the Democratic Party who do consistently win elections for major public office, the view that victory will come if we only speak more clearly from the left has disproportionately few supporters.

Unfortunately, given the mind-set of many of the issue-driven Democratic activists, this disinclination on the part of most officeholders to adopt the winning-through-louder-liberalism approach is taken not as our reasoned pragmatic judgment but as an indication of our lack of moral fiber. No factor is a source of greater mutual aggravation between these two elements of the party than the differences over what the ideologues describe as the officeholders' refusal or—when they are feeling charitable about our motives—our inability to "educate the voters" properly.

The need to educate the voters is the fallback position of those who, having seen unvarnished progressivism falter at the polls, nonetheless refuse to doubt its ultimate electoral efficacy. The problem, they say, is that liberal leaders—officeholders and candidates—haven't done a good enough job of educating the electorate. The voters' opposition to higher taxes, in this view, results not from their preference for hanging onto as much of their own money as possible but from the failure of liberal governors, senators, and congresspeople correctly to instruct them on the moral duties of citizenship. Strong popular support for policies intended to put thick walls between the average citizen and the average mugger result from the public's lack of understanding of the ravages of poverty and racism on young male psyches—which lack results in turn from the unwillingness of timid Democratic careerists to confront the prejudices of their constituents in a forthright manner.

Suggestions from those who have fought on behalf

of liberal principles in various legislative and electoral arenas that persuading the voters to change their minds on major public questions is often more easily advocated than accomplished are generally dismissed as transparent self-justifications. If you believe that, presented with the properly framed choice the people will always do the right thing, and that the policies you advocate are demonstrably in the public interest, it must then be the politicians' fault when things go badly.

This attitude gives rise to two sets of negative consequences. First, it exacerbates the feuding that plagues the Democratic Party's presidential chances. Second, it reenforces the fatal resistance to what we need to do: convince the voters that the values it thinks Democrats hold as a national party are not in fact the values which govern our behavior in office.

There are several obstacles confronting those who seek to educate voters—that is, to persuade large numbers of citizens to change their minds about important issues or about an entire set of issues or a party—and the job obviously gets harder as the subject becomes more encompassing. Citizens have jobs, families, hobbies, illnesses, chores, and a variety of other things that distract them from paying full attention to complex political discourses.

And even for those voters who do devote a good deal of attention to politics, there are problems for the politician in the moral-instructor mode. For one thing, a good many voters don't think highly of us. For some reason, many people who delight in pointing out how lowly politicians are regarded profess puzzlement that these self-same politicians are unsuccessful in persuading those who think poorly of them to change their opinions on very significant issues.

Moreover, the model of educating the voters that is applied almost always assumes that education is an uncompetitive sport. Why don't you just tell the voters X? activists implore us. How come you haven't pointed out Y? The answer very often is that we have sought to do just that, but that other politicians have been simultaneously arguing $X-5$ or $Y+13$, and that voters, in the limited time they devote to politics, and with their inclination to suspect politicians' motives, declined to accept everything we told them.

These obstacles are generic, confronting any political leader who seeks to instruct the electorate. For Democrats, particularly liberals, there is an even larger obstacle, which is our own special burden: the very reason we have to try to educate the voters about our basic values is the major barrier to our success in doing so. Voters do not submit passively to be educated in a political and ideological vacuum. They bring to their monitoring of the political debate all of their preconceptions and ideas about the political actors. Thus, they hear liberal arguments through a screen that predisposes them to believe that we Democrats are heedless of their tax money, embarrassed about America's role in the world, and strongly inclined to pander to minorities of various sorts.

The major educational task liberals face is to diseducate voters about our basic belief structure. Until we correct these misconceptions, our efforts at persuasion on specific issues or candidates will be severely handicapped.

Thus, my argument is not that we in elected office should not be trying to educate the voters; it is that this educational task will fail unless it is properly understood. Ever more eloquent repetitions of our rectitude can help make our case—as long as they refrain from implying that those voters who do not always agree with us are shortsighted bigots. But at this point the positive presentation of our position will not be enough—it is necessary, but not sufficient. What must be added is a systematic, sustained demonstration that our positions on issues grow logically from our commitment to the very same values as those held by the majority of Americans.

And here is where many of the left activists get off the educational train. For a variety of reasons, some strategic, some ideological, some attitudinal, and all of them wrong, many in our party strongly object to any effort to demonstrate that liberals are patriotic supporters of the free-enterprise system who think that hard work should be rewarded and violent criminals severely punished. (For those unfamiliar with intra-Democratic debates who may be skeptical of this assertion, I commend it to you as my best evidence: few things I have written will be as controversial to many of my best liberal friends.)

Why, these people ask angrily, must we engage in public attestations to our virtue just to satisfy our enemies. The short answer is so that we can win more elections. The longer version is that, partly because of our own mistakes, and partly because our opponents have been clever at exploiting them, our commitment to some of these basic values is questionable in the minds of voters whose support we need to win the presidency, and since we believe in these principles, our reluctance to say so on frequent public occasions has no effect except to reenforce these doubts.

But this need to repudiate the notsapostas does not mean that we should repudiate liberalism. One result of the reluctance of pragmatic liberals to disagree with our friends to the left is an intraparty vacuum, filled much too enthusiastically by Democratic ideologues of the right. The danger this presents was best stated by Mario Cuomo when he noted that some of the angrier elements within the Democratic Leadership Council want Democrats to plead guilty to political crimes we have not committed, thus compounding the problem of how we are perceived by swing voters.

This is why for some of us who agree that the Democratic nominating process has tilted too far left the notion of being rescued by the right wing of the DLC is like being on the *Lusitania* and being told that the *Ti-*

tanic has just been sent to rescue you. There was a move away from this unfortunate approach in 1991 by the elected officials who head the DLC, but too many of the staff of that organization remain as fixated on intra-party battles as their ideological mirror opposites. And their prescription that we move significantly rightward to recapture the presidency is wrong for four reasons: we shouldn't; we can't; it wouldn't work if we tried; and we don't have to.

The first of these arguments of course reflects my own ideological commitment. My purpose here is to demonstrate that mainstream Democratic commitments to social justice and economic fairness can form the basis of a successful presidential campaign, not to justify abandoning them. If it proves to be the case that only a moderate conservative can win the presidency, I will have to learn how to be happier in the loyal opposition.

But even Democrats more flexible on the issues than I am must understand the next problem with this viewpoint: it cannot be carried out successfully. I hope—and believe—that many activist Democrats can be persuaded of the wisdom of couching our basic principles in ways that better take into account American political reality. I do not think it would be possible to persuade them to abandon liberal goals.

Democratic presidential nominations have turned out as they have, after all, not because of some grand scheme of a few people, but because millions of Democratic voters have acted in a certain way. Given the sprawling nature of American political parties—as opposed to their more structured British counterparts—effecting any conscious change in party strategy at the national level is a difficult thing. A wholesale revision in its platform is usually impossible over any short run.

Third, even if it were both desirable and possible to move the unwieldy aggregation known as the Democratic Party noticeably rightward, the result would almost certainly be electoral losses, not gains. It is a good deal easier in politics to lose your friends than to win over your longtime enemies, and a Democratic Party that too closely resembled the Republicans would very probably suffer exactly that fate. Finally, the record of the electoral process as well as other evidence demonstrates that we do not have to move right to win.

The Democrats' Strengths

The most relevant part of our record is the fact that Democrats have, since 1968, continued to win a significant majority of partisan elections at every level below the presidency. Thus, my view that most voters, on balance, support Democratic positions on the issues involved in congressional, gubernatorial, and state legislative races rests on the assumption that they are basically rational in their voting choices. The inference that these voters support most of the policies advocated by those for whom they vote is strengthened by the fact that we are dealing here with a voting pattern that has persisted for many years, not just the results of two or three elections.

The second line of evidence for this view is public-opinion data. To ignore polling information in a discussion of what a large group of voters actually think would be an obvious error, but an equally grave if less obvious mistake would be to allow it alone to determine the question.

Polls are especially unreliable in giving information about issues, because they cannot measure what to elected officials is the critical factor—intensity of feeling. For example, there are union members who tend to agree with Democratic views on most issues before Congress, but whose anti-gun-control feelings are so much stronger than their other political opinions that they will vote for an anti-gun-control conservative over a pro-gun-control liberal with whom they agree on a longer list of issues.

Moreover, when issues are being surveyed, results will differ widely not only over time, but according to how questions are framed, what other information is given, what alternatives are posed, etc. My skepticism about polling on issues having been stated, it is nonetheless one relevant datum that on the vote-determining issues that divide the parties, the Democratic position on specific issues is the preferred one more often than not among this swing-voter group. More progressive taxation of the wealthy, expansion of medical care programs, more federal help for the homeless and for education, protection of American industries and workers from significant job loss to foreign competition, more vigorous government regulation of the environment and for consumer safety and protection— polls on these issues provide strong evidence that supporters of Democratic congressional and gubernatorial candidates know what they are doing.

Even better evidence comes from our recent governmental and political history.

Exhibit A is the 1990 budget negotiations and their aftermath. Because these efforts were about the entire federal budget, more than any other set of recent events they put the competing partisan views of government into contention. And both during and after this summit it was clear that the Democrats were having the better part of the political argument.

Two major differences divided the parties. On the revenue side the Republicans wanted lower capital gains and higher consumption taxes while the Democrats opposed any capital gains cuts and supported tax increases that would be paid mostly by the wealthy. There was, to the Republicans' disappointment, no difference between the parties on the amount of tax revenue to be raised, since the Democratic leadership had declined to support higher taxes until after President Bush publicly recanted his 1988 no-new-tax pledge. And, particularly relevant to my argument, this refusal also disappointed some Democrats who had been urging that we show the "courage" to make Democratic insistence on higher taxes a defining issue between the parties.

Had we accepted this viewpoint, President Bush would have been spared the embarrassment of asking America to unread his lips; instead, he could have entered budget negotiations as the defender of the taxpayer, and held out until the tax-hungry Democrats forced him to agree to revenue increases. Moreover, had the Democrats allowed this scenario to unfold, the ultimate tax package might well have been even less progressive than the one adopted. Given the dynamic of negotiations, if the very fact of a tax increase had been a major concession granted to the Democrats, the Republicans would have had more leverage in setting the specific terms of the increase: "Okay," the president would have argued, "I give in to your intransigence in favor of higher taxes, but only if you accept my version of the bill." But once there was agreement between the parties that taxes had to go up, the Democratic preference for higher taxes on the incomes of the wealthy was a clear political winner. Thus, if the Democrats had gone along with those who had been insisting that our party should have broken the budget deadlock by boldly proclaiming our preference for higher taxes, the public-policy result would have been somewhat worse from our standpoint, and the political results would have been a significant gain for the Republicans rather than one of the clearest Democratic political victories in a long time in this sort of contest.

On the expenditure side the issue was equally clearcut. The parties were again in agreement on totals, but the Republicans wanted higher military spending and lower domestic spending than the Democrats, especially in the area of medical care for the elderly. And the Democratic position was clearly the more popular one. Implicitly acknowledging that drastic domestic-spending cuts are an idea better praised in the abstract than advocated in the particular, the president was never eager to join the battle on this front. Thus, the record of confusion, hesitancy, and public reversals of position that plagued the administration during this period was not caused by disorganization but was the White House reaction to the unhappy fact that their preferred governmental strategy was politically unpopular.

Nor were congressional Republicans any more confident of their best course. During the budget debate in the spring of 1990, the House Republicans refused to use their opportunity to present either the president's budget or any variant thereof for a vote, understanding that the kind of program cuts required to reach the spending total they supported would have been politically unhealthy.

This recognition that they had taken the unpopular side of the budget issues explains why it was the

Republicans who began to complain about leaks during the negotiations. They understood that the Democratic sides of both the taxing and spending issues were far more appealing electorally, and their hope was that the two positions could be merged into a compromise product without either side having had to identify what preferences it brought to the process.

In fact, what at first pained the Democratic congressional leadership—their inability to get a majority in the House to accept the first compromise version of the budget—ultimately worked to the Democrats' advantage. The defeat of the first package was followed in the House by passage of a Democratic proposal that had a more progressive set of tax increases and a spending program that provided more domestic spending and less military money. Of the three budget packages voted on in the House during the fall of 1990, this was the only one to command any enthusiasm among Democrats. And nearly all Democrats welcomed the chance to point out the contrasts between the Democratic package and the two compromise versions. Even though the Democratic proposal, with its taxes on the wealthy and higher levels of domestic spending never progressed beyond House passage, Democrats who voted for it were able to cite it as an example of what we would have done if the Republicans hadn't used their control of the presidency to force us into the less popular compromise proposal that subsequently passed both Houses and was signed into law.

The political fallout from this dispute contributed to a Democratic showing in the 1990 elections that was better than had been expected. And the Democratic advantage on what became defined as fairness kept growing as 1991 began, to the point where it threatened—or promised—to transcend the gap between an issue and a value. That is, it seemed likely to Democrats and Republicans alike that by carrying over some of the unresolved issues from 1990 into the new year and focusing legislative attention on them, the Democrats had the opportunity to show the swing voters that we were, as a national party, superior to the Republicans on the basic value of equity for average Americans.

The president and his supporters began to counterattack on this front as 1991 began. For example, the Bush budget for fiscal 1992 featured a highly public attack on federal programs it denounced for subsidizing the rich, choosing programs where Republican strategists believed Democrats would be so tied to the recipient groups that we would have to defend every last unjustifiable subsidized penny. But just as that debate was being joined, the president benefited from a much more effective counter to the Democrats' budget gains—the popularity he gained from the great success of the war against Iraq.

This prevented the Democrats from building on the political advantages won in the budget fight, but it does not invalidate the point most relevant here: that the

Democratic position on this broad range of issues involved in the 1990 budget debate was understood by everyone involved in it to be the more popular one with the voters.

Nor is this the only hard evidence we have for the fact that Democratic positions on the specific issues are on balance the ones with the greater electoral appeal. Exhibit B on this point is *The Triumph of Politics,* published in 1986 by David Stockman, who more than anyone in recent years tried to wage a frontal assault on the collection of benefit programs, subsidies, and regulations that make up the welfare state

Stockman fought consistently against the liberal economic agenda in Congress in the seventies, and he took the job as director of the Office of Management and Budget under Ronald Reagan prepared to wage the battle from a more commanding height. He soon found, as he wrote in his book, that these liberal programs expanded because the voters wanted them to expand:

> . . . my anti-welfare state theory . . . rested on the illusion that the will of the people was at drastic variance with the actions of the politicians.
>
> But the political history of the past five years [1981–86] mostly invalidates that proposition. We have had a tumultuous national referendum on everything in our half-trillion-

dollar welfare state budget. . . . I am as quali-
fied as anyone to discern the verdict. . . .

Despite their often fuzzy rhetoric and
twisted rationalizations, congressmen and
senators ultimately deliver what their con-
stituencies demand. . . .

What you see done in the halls of the
politicians may not be wise, but it is the only
real and viable definition of what the electorate wants. (pp. 376–77)

This of course counters those who argue that the electoral and governmental triumphs of Ronald Reagan
demonstrate that the conservative position on the issues is politically irresistible when it is correctly presented. As Stockman acknowledges, and as the record
makes clear, Reagan's big victories were over what he
so successfully dramatized as the excesses of liberalism, not its essence.

BOTH IN HIS DEFEAT of Jimmy Carter and in
his legislative successes in 1981, Ronald Reagan benefited from a perception that he brilliantly helped to
shape: that the network of subsidies, benefits, and regulations the Democrats had put together over the
preceding fifty years had gotten dangerously out of
control. Reagan won support from voters because of
their view that the welfare programs were shot through

with fraud, waste, and abuse, and that consumer, safety, and environmental regulations had become unduly burdensome on the economy. House Democrats were unable to resist the deep program cuts embodied in the Gramm-Latta budget bill of 1981 because the voters saw it as a vehicle to make drastically needed reforms. This was the corrective that would curtail the free ride of welfare queens, middle-class college students on food stamps, and superfluous bureaucrats eager to harass honest workers and businesspeople. But the voters were not ready to go beyond cutting away the fringe of abuse to making drastic reductions in the programs themselves.

This is the major reason why, after his extraordinary legislative successes of 1981, Ronald Reagan's subsequent legislative record was largely one of frustration. Even on the tax side, the first major tax cut in 1981 was also the last of the Reagan era. Thereafter, Reagan signed into law additional tax bills, but they consisted of several tax increases and one revenue-neutral tax overhaul.

Two examples help make the point. Distaste for excessive regulation was a strong element in Reagan's own ideology, and the image of Jimmy Carter as an interfering fussbudget helped defeat him in 1980. But as it became clear that such Reagan appointees as James Watt in the Interior Department and Anne Gorsuch Burford at the Environmental Protection Administration intended not to make the programs under their jurisdiction run more efficiently but instead seriously to reduce their scope, they became clear political liabilities and were pushed out the door.

An even more dramatic shift occurred regarding programs for the elderly. Starting from his advocacy of cutbacks in Social Security and Medicare early in his term, Reagan had by his 1984 reelection campaign reached the point where he complained of unfairness at any suggestion that he shared conservative opinions about the need to trim these programs. Reagan's budgets did consistently propose cuts in Medicare, but these were never very seriously defended, and their presence was always taken as one of the major political liabilities that made Republicans in Congress shy away from pushing presidential budgets.

The third exhibit is the presidential campaign of 1988. George Bush was the conservative candidate for president. He was also, on his insistence, the education candidate for president as well as the environmental candidate. He vigorously and effectively used such conservative themes as tough treatment of criminals, enforced respect for the flag, free enterprise, and a strong America. But he not only avoided the right-wing position on many specific issues, he often embraced variants of what has been the liberal side of the debate. This led to a major inconsistency between his most striking reaffirmation of conservative purity—the no-new-tax pledge—and his seemingly liberal promise of more government activity on behalf of schools, the environment, and children. What the formula lacked in logic it more than made up for in electoral appeal.

Ironically, George Bush showed a better understanding of the political strength of these traditional liberal positions than Michael Dukakis. The latter's decision to eschew campaigning on issues—announced in his acceptance speech assertion that "this campaign is about competence, not ideology"—left him with no weapons to use against the Republican attack on his values. Only when Dukakis began emphasizing traditional Democratic stands on the issues very late in the campaign did he begin to win back lost ground.

Admittedly, the arguments I have been drawing from this history to buttress my point deal mostly with domestic programs, where the Democratic advantage is the strongest. In the social area the record is mixed, with conservative positions more popular on the crime issues and in some aspects of freedom of expression. Offsetting this, however, is the dramatic shift on the question of abortion, which was once seen as a great boon to conservative political hopes and is now one of their most difficult problems. And the Democrats profit politically much more often than not when the issue at stake is the right of women to be free of historic forms of discrimination.

On international issues the Republicans have had the better side of the debate, but here too the advantages are divided. Conservatives have done better in the past fifteen years when the question has been the use of military force by the United States, but the Democratic position on foreign economic matters has had more popular appeal. And the question of spending on the military, as I will argue later, is evolving.

In summary, my argument is not that the Democratic position is the more electorally advantageous on every issue, or even that there are not times, as in 1980, when the voters prefer the conservative side of most specific policy debates. But given the predominance most of the time in our politics on the complex of economic and regulatory issues, on which the liberal side has our greatest popular advantage, and the roughly even division of political pluses and minuses between the parties on other issues—Democratic domination of congressional, gubernatorial, and legislative elections is not accidental.

Neither is it the skewed result of a flawed system. The last objection that I have to deal with here is that the bifurcated electoral pattern of the past twenty-five years represents the inconsistency between the policy preferences of a majority of voters on the one hand and the distorted outcome of a defective political system on the other—what David Stockman derides as "the notion that Washington amounts to a puzzle palace on the Potomac, divorced from the genuine desires of the voters. . . .

Stockman summarizes it as the viewpoint that

"somehow . . . manages to divine a great unwashed mass of the citizenry demanding the opposite of the spending agendas presented by the Claude Peppers, the homebuilders' lobby, and the other hired guns . . ." It is a proposition, Stockman notes, that "constitutes more myth than truth."

Of course, in the unromantic world of political debate even myths need a logical structure to be servicable. Ideology can lead people to accept a convenient explanation of unpleasant facts, but only if there is a plausible one handy. In the case of conservatives trying to explain why a rightward-leaning electorate so regularly chooses leftward-leaning senators, representatives, and governors, the answer is the bewitching power of incumbency to lead voters astray.

Incumbent officeholders, the argument goes, have so rigged the system that liberals survive in office not because they better represent voter preferences than their conservative challengers but because of the insuperable advantages incumbents enjoy.

To begin with, this fails entirely on its own terms to explain why Democrats continue to dominate Congress despite Republican presidential victories. If the advantages of incumbency were the reason Democrats still controlled Congress, this would mean a steady erosion in the margin of Democratic control, as Republicans drew on their popularity to win a majority of the seats that opened up as incumbents died, retired, or sought other offices. The Democratic majority would be dropping steadily and the Republican success rate for open seats would be substantial.

The facts are completely the opposite. In 1980, thanks to the anti-Democratic trend that swept out Jimmy Carter, Ronald Reagan took office with a Republican majority in the Senate of 54–46, and with one of the largest Republican House minorities in recent times—192 to 243 Democrats.

According to the theory that Democrats have held power only because Democratic incumbents have staved off the conservative tide, by now there would be a heavier Republican majority in the Senate and probably a majority in the House as well. Instead, the Democrats have made substantial gains in both Houses. This happened because Democrats did better than Republicans in every possible kind of election. Democrats scored a net gain of five seats in elections to fill the spots of retiring members. Democrats won twelve of twenty-two seats created by redistricting. And despite the arguments for incumbent invulnerability, forty-seven Democratic challengers defeated incumbent Republicans, while only twenty-five Republicans ousted sitting Democrats.

Consequently, after five elections in which the conservative tide had the chance to improve the Republican standing, the Democrats now have a hundred-seat majority in the House—twice what it was in 1981. This has hardly been the product of inertia. Speaker Thomas

Foley has noted that if the Republicans held today every seat they had held at some point in the 1980s, they would in fact have a majority today.

Nor do these figures exhaust the weaknesses of the incumbency argument. If it is to serve the ideological purposes to which it is being put, this line of reasoning would have to explain as well the continuing Democratic preponderance in governors' offices, and it is even more patently inadequate here. Few people argue that incumbency is any great advantage for governors. Proponents of the "incumbency makes them do it" explanation more often denounce the electoral benefits of officeholding than describe them, probably because when enumerated they appear far less impressive. But when the advantages are listed, they clearly have less application to governors than to members of Congress. Indeed, in difficult economic times, being a sitting chief executive is as likely to be a handicap politically as a great boon. And in fact, in every election there are frequent defeats of incumbent governors and a considerable number of partisan shifts at the statehouse level. But through all of the defeats of incumbents and changes in party control of governorships in the eighties, one fact remained constant—a Democratic numerical edge that simply cannot be accounted for by any variant of the incumbency argument. It is not only governorships where the incumbency argument lacks even surface statistical plausibility. Sitting senators during the past decade have had a much lower reelection rate than members of the House. From 1980 through 1990, about 15 percent of senators seeking reelection were defeated. The inherent advantages of the already-elected do very little to explain Democratic control of the Senate for most of this period.

I do not object to the assertion that incumbency is an advantage in many—but by no means all—elections. My point is that this phenomenon is neither as widespread, as pernicious, nor as recent as it has come to be described, and most particularly that it is a relatively neutral ideological factor that cannot bear the heavy weight conservatives have sought to load on it.

What the feared "incumbency" factor comes down to is that voters, having once selected someone to represent them in a legislative district, tend strongly to vote for him or her again two or four years later, especially if the legislator in question has been diligent about staying in touch with those voters, paying attention to their opinions, and acting as an advocate for their interests. Why this should be considered by some to be a terrible thing is baffling—as a legislator I must be in the only profession in the world where a high degree of consumer satisfaction is taken as a sign that something is radically wrong.

But, the argument goes, what I am describing is the benign system of yesteryear. What was a likelihood that incumbents would be reelected has now become a certainty, and not because of natural political forces but because of manipulations of the system by and for entrenched legislators.

It is true that a higher percentage of incumbents win reelection these days to the U.S. House. But the major reason for this trend has very little to do with campaign spending, or congressional mailing privileges, or any other factor over which House members have direct influence.

The reason fewer incumbent House members lose elections today than was the case twenty to thirty years ago is that the American people have moved away from voting along party lines.

Historically, most congresspeople who have been defeated for reelection have lost as part of a national trend against their party. In 1946 many Democrats lost their seats in the postwar Republican surge. In 1964 the Goldwater candidacy swept many otherwise invulnerable Republicans out of office. Two years later anti-Johnson feelings unseated large numbers of Democrats again. It was the Republicans' turn to get defeated after Watergate in 1974, and the Democrats took their lumps—although in lesser numbers—in the Reagan year of 1980.

What is characteristic of these years in which large numbers of incumbents lost their seats is that nearly all the losses were in one party. That is, rarely in recent history have incumbent congresspeople lost in primaries in any large number, nor have there been randomly distributed defeats of large numbers of Democrats and Republicans. The pattern is as I described it above—having once voted for a candidate, most voters are likely to vote for that candidate again, especially if he or she has the minimal good sense once in office to be responsive to them. Consequently, for the overwhelming majority of legislators, the only serious threat to reelection came when the voters wanted to express dissatisfaction with the party to which those legislators belonged.

This has not historically been true of governorships. Here the pattern of incumbent defeats cutting across party lines is much more common, because chief executives have many more opportunities than legislators to get into political trouble. Legislators are judged by their advocacy; executives are more likely to be held accountable for outcomes.

The decline in the tendency of Americans to vote along party lines has therefore had little impact on the reelection rate of incumbent governors. And it has had only some impact on senators, because the larger size and greater diversity of interests of most states as compared to House districts makes them politically more complicated to represent, and thus more likely to oust incumbents. But it has led to the increase that has been noted in the ability of House members to stay in office.

This is not to deny that representatives do what they can to make their chances even better. And some of these most recent efforts do work against electoral fairness—abuses of congressional mailing privileges had become too frequent by 1990, and while some reforms have been adopted in these practices, even tighter controls are in order. But other congressional practices that are sometimes decried for undercutting electoral fairness seem to me neither undesirable nor changeable—do critics really think American democracy would function better if congresspeople did not visit their districts regularly? And the argument that incumbent financing advantages are the key factor in insulating officeholders from effective challenge is rebutted by the fact that the offices where the most money is required to win—statewide contests for senator and governor—are the ones in which challengers are the most competitive.

In any case, whatever one's views on the role of incumbency, it is clearly not a significant part of the reason that Democrats have continued to dominate nonpresidential offices in the era of Republican presidencies.

How to Fix It

THE question facing liberal Democrats is how to do in presidential elections what we are generally successful in doing in nonpresidential contests. How do we translate the broad public support that exists for our position on the issues into victory on election day?

In recent years, four issues have been particularly damaging to our presidential chances: national security, taxes, crime, and racial discrimination.

Our task is to present positions on these issues that reflect the public-policy views of most Democrats while appealing to enough of the swing votes to win.

This is a complicated effort, in practice as well as in theory. In the United Kingdom, with the centralized political parties and tight party structures, there is at least a mechanism for doing this. Thus, Neil Kinnock was able at a series of Labor party conferences to move his party away from the militant leftist posture that doomed it to constant defeat. No such mechanism exists in our country, so no single act or series of acts can make any given view the policy of the Democratic party.

What those who share my view can do is to articulate our view of how Democrats should frame the issues on the national level, and then work hard to support candidates who advocate this approach. This means pragmatic liberals must be more willing than we have been in the past to explain why we differ with many of our ideologically militant friends. It means that liberal Democrats in public office who understand that we cannot win the presidency until we adopt a different approach must be willing to get more deeply involved in the presidential nominating process on behalf of this view.

In the following sections, I outline an approach to these troublesome issues which I believe preserves the moral core of liberal positions while jettisoning much of the unpopular baggage we have allowed them to accumulate. What is central here is that liberals have to do this, not because we should be inclined to compromise away our basic commitments, but rather because we are serious enough about them to want them to become public policy. We simply cannot be effective on behalf of those things we care about if we continue to lose the single most important institution that has an effect on them—the presidency.

.   .   .

AT THE presidential level, no issue has been more important in the postwar years than national security. Since 1968, no issue has cost the Democrats more heavily. In the future, no issue holds more promise for democratic advantage.

The reason is that George Bush insists that despite the complete collapse of the worldwide Communist empire, American taxpayers should continue to spend massive sums to help our wealthy European and Asian allies feel more secure, even though no one, including them, can point to any serious threats to their security, and despite the fact that they have become our economic equals, well able to spend more on their own defense, but wisely declining to do so as long as they can get Uncle Sam to pick up their military tab. Indeed, the single most effective thing we could do to diminish any Japanese or West European sense of vulnerability would be to announce that we will supply them in the future with as much military protection as they are willing to pay us to provide. As all of us free-marketeers understand, people usually demand more of a free good than of one they have to pay for. Confronted with a bill for the full cost of the American forces now defending Western Europe and East Asia, our allies would almost certainly feel safer, and in need of far less protection than they claim they've needed.

As a result of George Bush's insistence that we continue to make an annual gift of well over $150 billion in security assistance to our wealthy allies, what is an important opportunity to improve the quality of life in America has become an equally striking opportunity for the Democratic Party to reestablish primacy at the presidential level.

The Cold War is over. America has won. And as the winners, Americans are entitled to a victory dividend—the right to spend some of the vast sums that for forty-five years have gone toward containing Communism instead of on our pressing domestic needs. In recent years we have been spending about $320 billion per year in 1991 dollars on our national security, including the defense and intelligence budgets. Let us assume, as I do not, that all of this was necessary, that about 70 percent of it was for deterring Communism, and that the Communist threat at the end of 1991 was as great as one-third what it used to be; that still allows for an annual savings of $150 billion. Given the vastness of our military might, qualitatively and quantitatively, and the total dissolution of the Warsaw Pact, and the weakening if not the total dismemberment of the Soviet Union, we can save more than $150 billion every year from our current level of defense and intelligence spending without sacrificing our standing as by far the strongest nation in the world, or jeopardizing our ability to defend any vital national interest.

Even before the August 1991 implosion of the So-

viet Union, George Bush acknowledged the most relevant part of this argument when he told a West Point
audience that "for more than four decades America's
energies were focused on containing the threat to the
free world from forces of Communism," and that the
Cold War that had required that focus had ended hap-
pily for our side.

What George Bush resists is allowing Americans to
enjoy the fruits of this victory. He has decided to be the
exact mirror opposite of an earlier Republican
George—the late Senator George Aiken, whose response to the trauma of Vietnam was to urge that
America declare victory and get out. Where the matter
of America's defense of Western Europe and much of
Asia is concerned, George Bush's position is that we
should ignore victory and stay in. It is this adamant
insistence by President Bush that we continue to spend
on national security at levels only marginally below
those of the Cold War that creates an opportunity for
the Democratic Party. What the Republicans now advocate, behind the leadership of their president, is that
Americans should continue to shoulder a grossly disproportionate share of the responsibility for world
order; that the American taxpayer should support a
level of national security spending that is from two to
six times as great a percentage of our gross national
product as that undertaken by our wealthy European
and Japanese allies, and that we should accept this
additional burden as the "price of leadership." What's

more, this view holds that in bilateral and multilateral economic relations, America, as the free world's political leader must defer to our allies to some extent. If we expect them to follow our political lead, the argument has gone, it is only natural that we have to give some in the nonpolitical areas—of which, of course, economics is paramount.* Joseph Nye notes in his book *Bound to Lead* that deference to our allies on economic issues has been a characteristic of America's efforts to preserve our global political leadership position.

The alternative view—clearly becoming the consensus position among Democrats at the end of 1991—is that America should maintain a strong nuclear deterrent, retain the capacity to intervene in trouble spots where weak nations might be threatened by aggression, and be well able to defend our own vital interests—but that we need not spend a significantly higher percentage of our GNP on defense than do Britain, Germany, or France. And it holds that while we have both a moral obligation and an enlightened self-interest in alleviating the poverty that plagues much of the third world, we have a right to treat the prosperous nations of Europe and Asia as equals: we should neither impose on them nor defer to them economically in the name of global security.

BUT GEORGE BUSH'S reluctance to let Americans have a genuine victory dividend is not the only precondition for the Democrats' being able to win back much of what we have lost politically on this issue. It is also essential that we use this as the chance to show the electorate that we have, finally and decisively, unlearned the bad old habits of our post-1968 presidential politics, and freed ourselves from the self-imposed tyranny of the notsapostas. If we allow our debate on how America should respond to our victory in the Cold War to be dominated by fear of offending the sensibilities of our activists on the left, we may not only not gain on this issue, we could find ourselves at even greater political disadvantage.

There are three different ways in which politicians can make the case for a substantial reduction in what Americans pay for the military defense of what we called the free world at a time when we had an obviously unfree one for purposes of comparison.

The first is the one most amenable to the left in the Democratic Party, and it picks up where the antiwar rhetoric of the Vietnam War days left off. To many in the ideological wing of the party, the end of the Cold War means an end to an era when America used the threat of Communism to impose itself on much of the rest of the world, usually for no good purpose. For one part of this group the United States not only exaggerated the Communist threat, we essentially created it—first by threatening behavior of our own, and then by distorted descriptions of Soviet reality. (This particular wing of the movement was, however, seriously weakened politically and intellectually by the Soviet leadership's break with the past in the nineties. It is hard to fight for the innocence of a nation that has just pled guilty to the charges.)

Yet it is not simply those who blame the United States for the Cold War who would have the Democratic Party put our worst foot forward here. Some of those who have not the slightest sympathy for Stalin's behavior in the postwar years nonetheless take a harshly critical view of this country's foreign policy as neoimperialist, unduly militaristic, racist, or rooted in a desire to defend profiteering by multinational corporations.

And, the post-1968 rules being in effect, the problem for Democrats is not just those who believe this, but those who are wary of offending or alienating those who believe this. As I noted in Part One, one of the most destructive of the notsapostas has been the rule that liberals were not supposed to talk loudly of the obvious moral superiority of the American system to the one in the Eastern bloc, lest we fan the flames of excessive nationalism. In its current form that view holds that we are notsaposta make the obvious point that the collapse of the Soviet bloc in the face of an American-led resistance to it is a triumph for freedom in the world. As long as moderates observe this notsaposta, swing voters will get the message that Democrats welcome the Communist collapse primarily because it allows America to stop imposing its military and economic might on a world that doesn't want it. We will also be seen as denigrating the U.S. military as a wasteful, bloated establishment which has succeeded more by unlimited spending and brute strength than by its skills. This approach will win us very few votes.

A second basis for insisting on a substantial roll-back of America's global role comes from the believers in the inevitable decline of any single great power. This argument has clearly been complicated in many ways by the fact that the Soviet empire fell apart before the predicted decline of the United States. But there are still people in the "America-is-in-decline school" who will argue that our opportunity to retrench has come just in time to allow us to avoid the terrible consequences of imperial overstretch. To George Bush's insistence that we maintain our far-flung military role as the price of leadership, they respond that we are unable to do so, that America simply cannot afford to play this role, and that if we try, we will go the way of empires past, and our own society will irrevocably decay.

These two arguments—that America has been a bad influence on the world and that the world has been a debilitating influence on America—are not mutually exclusive, and they are often made simultaneously, particularly by those who are disenchanted with America and are temperamentally and intellectually more comfortable deploring America than celebrating it. Alone or in combination they are politically unwise.

The first argument is the worst for us politically,

with its direct connection to the attitudes of the protesters of the sixties. But the decline argument hurts us as well—it evokes the negativism about America that the swing voters resent in the attitudes of the left. Talking negatively about America is not a good way to get proud Americans to vote for you. This does not mean that all criticism be muted; it means that when the specific criticisms are put in a framework that denigrates American society, the reaction of many voters will be adverse.

Fortunately, there is a third way to justify a redirection of $150 billion dollars a year from national security to domestic needs, one that is politically far more effective in rallying support than the two options I have just sketched above. Even better, it is the position that best represents the views of the mainstream liberals who compose the dominant Democratic position in Congress, and who must be mobilized if we are to win the presidency. This argument deliberately refers to a victory dividend rather than a peace dividend. Words take on political shadings over the years. To many swing voters supporters of a peace dividend are part of a movement that has frequently blamed America for many of the ills in the world, has reduced the role of our military, and may be naive about the need for us to use force in defense of our legitimate interests.

"Victory dividend" in contrast has about it an air of triumph—of pride in America's accomplishment of bringing about the defeat of Communism as a world system, and in protecting much of the world against the Soviet Union when it was an aggressive power. I believe it is the right term because it makes clear that the decision to bring home more than $150 billion per year to spend on our economy—on everything from better television sets to better health care—is just that: our freely taken decision. It should not be the Democrats' position that America is withdrawing much of its military from around the world because the world has suffered from our presence, or that America is so weak that we can no longer afford the cost of our commitment.

The liberal Democratic position is and should be that America has done much of the job it set out to do in 1945: now that Communism is a spent force, Eastern Europe has been liberated, Western Europe and Japan are prosperous and democratic, we can apply most of the resources we dedicated to accomplishing these tasks to other purposes, including fighting poverty in the third world and working on behalf of human rights everywhere. Most of all we can use vast sums that have been freed up by our international victory to alleviate difficult problems at home.

The starting point of the case for the victory dividend is precisely the one George Bush made in a recent speech to Congress: for forty-five years America made the deterrence of Communist aggression the greatest single focus of our policy. In pursuit of that goal we spent our tax dollars on the most comprehensive worldwide military apparatus in history, supported by an equally extensive intelligence network, human and technical. Only Social Security has consumed a larger share of America's budget in the postwar years than the money we have spent directly on defense against Communism.

Overall, this is a record of which Americans should be very proud, and this is a pride liberal Democrats should make clear we share. When World War II ended, America undertook an unusually generous policy by world and historical standards. Not only did we soon begin a massive program of aid to our former allies, we also began working hard and effectively, at considerable expense to ourselves, on the economic and political rehabilitation of our former enemies. Of course, America made errors in the intervening years; and of course our efforts were motivated in substantial part by self-interest in containing the threat of Communism. But we are still entitled to point proudly to our role in helping Germany and Japan progress to the point where they are not only extremely prosperous but genuinely democratic in a way that neither had ever been before for any substantial period of time.

Through this period America provided money, troops, and military equipment for the common defense and also sacrificed its own economic interests on behalf of allied solidarity. As Joseph Nye notes, ''The United States often subordinated its economic interests during the period of the supposed Pax Americana because it was concerned about the high politics of the global balance and the challenge of Soviet power" (*Bound to Lead*, p. 90).

But two essential facts have changed in the last five years. Most important, the hostile, monolithic Communist bloc is now not very hostile, completely fractionalized, and in fact in what used to be its most fearsome locus, not even Communist. Second, the allies to whom we have given so much protection in the past forty-five years are no longer the impoverished, defenseless nations that emerged shattered from the trauma of World War II. They are still our allies; yet now they are also our economic equals and our increasingly successful economic competitors.

In other words, the policy America set forth in the postwar years, beginning with the Truman administration, has been as completely successful as it is possible to be in a complicated world. And we can now enjoy the benefits of that victory.

With the demise of any threat of a Warsaw Pact land invasion of Europe, the need for a massive American presence on the Continent is gone. With the demise of the Soviet Union as a threatening power, Japan's needs for an American defense subsidy that in 1991 amounted to about $5 billion annually is also gone. Even in South Korea, which as of 1991 still faced one of the few unreconstructed, repressive Communist regimes left, we can safely reduce our heavy troop strength. South Korea is larger than North Korea, with a bigger and better economy. In the absence of any likely support for the North Koreans from its erstwhile Communist big brothers, a substantially reduced American troop presence should suffice to keep things calm.

In the strategic nuclear area, the need for vastly sophisticated and expensive nuclear delivery systems has greatly diminished, and it is hard to see the need for a full-blown strategic defense system to protect us against a no longer likely hail of Soviet ICBMs. Nor do we need the worldwide network of bases we have maintained for forty-five years, a network that was put in place primarily as part of a global garrison aimed at a global Communist threat.

We should maintain an invulnerable nuclear deterrent with submarines playing a major role. We should continue to have the most powerful army, navy, and air force in the world along with bases that would allow easy access to trouble spots such as the Middle East. But it would be the world's strangest—and most expensive—coincidence if it turned out that the massive amount of force we needed to contain a worldwide Communist threat led by a mighty superpower is almost the same as what we need to help our allies protect themselves now that this force has shrunk by several orders of magnitude and has no realistic promise of resuming its former role.

I stress this last point because I recognize that, given the political facts of life for the past twenty-five years, liberal Democrats urging large military cuts have to prove that our position is based on a hard assessment of reality and not on wishful global thinking. So it is essential for me to demonstrate conclusively the factual basis of this argument.

First, since 1945, except during the Korean and Vietnam wars, the biggest single chunk of America's military spending has gone to NATO, i.e., to preventing a Soviet-led land attack with Poland, Hungary, East Germany, Czechoslovakia, Bulgaria, and sometimes Albania or Romania joining the Communist hordes in overrunning the West. By 1990 it was clear that there was simply no chance of this in any foreseeable future. In fact, it seems to me that it has been a very long time indeed since any Russian general would have decided it was safe to give arms to Polish or Hungarian troops and then turn his back on them, much less to rely on them to help him invade France or Denmark. By the end of 1991, no rational human being thought this was very likely.

Today the only place you can find any support for the possibility that the defunct Warsaw Pact might rise again and invade the West was in America's military budget. In 1991, spurred on by President Bush, a nearly unanimous bloc of House Republicans rebuffed the efforts of a majority of Democrats to make a cut of several billion dollars in the military budget allocated to provide American troops for NATO. This, of course, was at the same time President Bush was explaining to the Europeans that American budgetary constraints kept us from providing any significant financial assistance to the former Russian satellites struggling toward freedom. In other words, the United States couldn't afford to help Poland in its march to democracy because we were still spending billions making sure that the Poles didn't join in an invasion of Belgium.

Second, even within what is now the former Soviet Union, no outcome seems remotely likely to return us to the height of the Cold War. No one can be sure that repression will not return to some parts of what was the Soviet bloc; but there is no likelihood that any such regime or regimes will seek to ride to power on a platform of once again starving the civilian side of the Soviet economy in order to keep a military machine in high hear. And there is virtually no chance that they would be successful if they did try. Conservative analysts have long told us to look at the capabilities of a potential enemy and not to be lulled by what we think are good intentions. It is now obvious that presenting a sustained military threat to a superpower like the United States is beyond the physical capacity of the Soviet Union—either as a whole or in its parts—and almost certainly beyond its political capacity as well. Finally, it seems clear that any such effort to turn the Soviet Union into a genuine superpower again would be a sufficiently difficult and drawn-out process as to give us plenty of lead time to respond, should all of my contentions prove wrong. It cannot be argued that we will somehow, with our great economic and technical strength, be unable to increase our forces in the future if there is some terrible reversal of events in Russia-Kazakhstan-Byelorussia-et al.

There are, it is true, other Communist powers. The largest by far is the People's Republic of China, a nation President Bush has been ardently courting. The president has the power, through his veto, to retain China's status as a most favored nation in trade, but one price he pays for achieving this is to forfeit any real chance of using the specter of Chinese Communist hordes to boost our military spending beyond the levels I am advocating. The North Koreans continue to be a threat, but, as I noted, they are no stronger than the South Koreans. About one-quarter of the American troop strength now in South Korea would suffice for its security needs, and would provide us with about 27,000 troops for which we would have no further need.

But what about other threats to the peace, apart from Communist aggression? What about the Saddam Husseins of the world? The short answer is that at a military expenditure level of $150 billion (in 1991 dollars) the United States would possess the military capacity to defeat any conceivable enemy or combination of enemies. Iraq is a good example. Saddam Hussein's continued hold on power reminds us that this is a very imperfect world—that despite a good deal of progress, there are still people running countries who, in an ideal world, wouldn't be allowed to drive cars. But the United States is so strong a power in both the amount and quality of our weapons that half of what we now have is still more than we are ever likely to need.

Iraq was, according to the Pentagon, the fourth-largest military power in the world and its armed forces were decimated by American troops in a very brief period. Nor did the United States have to use all or even most of its military resources to accomplish this. Well over a million American troops stayed at their posts in Europe, Japan, South Korea, the Philippines, and elsewhere during this period. With the demise of the Russian-led military threat, Iraq apparently represented the next-greatest source of hostile armed force. The experience of the Gulf War makes clear that our choice is not between keeping American strength at current levels or facing global impotence.

It is true that American forces weren't the only forces in Iraq. But we did provide the greatest bulk of the firepower and personnel. And the help we received from our allies should only strengthen the case for cutting our defense budget. The more we share the burden, the less the cost of leadership remains exclusively ours.

Two other points are relevant to this discussion of the war in Iraq. Some conservatives have argued that our effort in Iraq only succeeded because the Reagan defense buildup had prevailed over liberal objections. That is simply wrong. There were serious disputes over military spending levels over the last ten years, with Democrats pushing for lower numbers than Republicans. But in terms of American forces needed to confront the Soviet Union, the debates in Congress were about amounts of marginal significance. Since Harry Truman's time, there has been a strong bipartisan consensus on keeping a level of American nuclear strength sufficient to deter the Soviets. Certainly, many Democrats opposed expensive excesses like the B-2 bomber, the MX missile, and the exotic aspects of antimissile defense. But never was there less than overwhelming Democratic support for a fully functional force of bombers with nuclear weapons; trident submarines; and a solid land-based missile system. Democrats also backed the drive to oppose Soviet aggression by conventional means. American military support for the resistance fighters in Afghanistan had nearly unanimous support from congressional Democrats from the start of that war in 1979.

Most of the weapons used in the victory over Iraq were not the center of great debate in the 1980s. The Gulf War showed the high quality of many sophisticated American weapons, weapons that had received overwhelming bipartisan support in Congress. The Republican right wing tried to take credit for the success of the Patriot antimissile defense system, one of the high points of the American military effort, by claiming it was the result of President Reagan's plans for the Strategic Defense Initiative. But the campaign failed because it was so far from the truth. Since the Patriot long predated Ronald Reagan's SDI speech, was a totally different weapons system, and had a very different purpose from the grand design of SDI, this argument soon disappeared.

The second charge liberals must dispel is the accusation that opposition to the war demonstrated anew that liberals have badly overreacted to Vietnam and oppose the use of America's force even when it is both morally justified and effective. Confronting this argument is especially important for liberals; it is a very clear example of the price we pay in the center if we worry excessively about the emotional temperature of our left.

This does not mean that liberals who voted against the war should try to pretend that we didn't. Quick conversions blatantly motivated by politics rarely work, fortunately. So we need to explain in a coherent, unapologetic way, why we voted not to go to war in January 1991.

My own experience in the winter and early spring of last year brought the issues into focus. Along with virtually all of my liberal Democratic colleagues, I was appalled by Saddam Hussein's aggression against Kuwait, and strongly supported President Bush's dispatch of American troops to Saudi Arabia to block any further Iraqi advance. Again, along with nearly all of my colleagues, I fully supported strong measures against

Iraq, including the threat of force, if necessary, to end the occupation of Kuwait. From the outset of the crisis, most liberal Democrats fully supported the American stance that Iraqi aggression was illegal, that the world had an obligation to aid Kuwait, and that force would be justified at some point if no other means prevailed. In taking these positions, I and others were clearly rejecting much of the viewpoint on this issue held by many to our left both in and out of the Democratic ranks. We were affirming the moral right of our country to take the lead in opposing aggression, contrary to those who argue that America's own record is so morally flawed that it should not take any military action abroad. Second, we were affirming that a lack of respect for human rights in a country that is being unfairly attacked is not a reason for standing aside and allowing it to be overrun.

The lack of democracy in Kuwait was, of course, an oft-cited argument by the left against our military effort. But this is an argument most liberal Democrats in Congress had rejected in August, when we supported troops for the Saudis. While I am not an expert in the degrees of oppression in Arab states, my clear impression is that in every category of human rights Saudi Arabia is even more deficient than Kuwait.

Unlike some critics of the Bush policy, congressional Democrats were clearly saying that America had the moral right to go to the aid of undemocratic Arab states that were being threatened by Saddam Hussein. And a majority of us agreed as well that force would ultimately be justified.

Where we differed with the president was over when war was justified. Many of us believed and still do that before you send the young people of your country to kill or be killed, you are obligated to exhaust the alternatives. And we felt—as I still do—that the president had not done that. Sanctions were in effect for far too short a period to have any impact, so we will never know if they would have helped. Ironically, after the war ended, the president who had been skeptical of sanctions in 1990 became their most ardent advocate, arguing for a very harsh set of economic restrictions on Iraq to force Saddam out of power. Our argument gains strength from this: if it was reasonable for the president to argue in 1991 that sanctions could force Saddam Hussein to give up his job, why was it out of the question that similar sanctions could not persuade him to withdraw from Kuwait.

In addition, while many of us enthusiastically supported the effort President Bush made to internationalize the effort against Iraq, particularly his skillful and important use of the United Nations, we feared that support from our allies would be largely verbal. My view was that American participation in a genuinely multilateral effort to expel the Iraqis was both fairer to Americans and likelier to succeed quickly than what I feared would be a largely American effort.

In the end, the president, spurred by Congress, did do a better job than I had expected in getting international help, particularly of the financial kind. And even more relevant was America's unexpectedly swift victory with fewer casualties on our side than had been expected.

These were the views I expressed in my congressional district in the immediate aftermath of the war, to a constituency that like most others in America was by war's end very supportive of the president's position. I had expected some opposition, given that I had voted against the war, spoken against it on the floor of the House, and helped organize the adoption of a resolution in the House insisting that no military action could be launched without prior congressional approval.

But I got very little, primarily, I believe, because I had made clear that my disagreement with President Bush on the specific decision to go to war in January did not mean that I was taking an anti-American stance overall. Most voters are perfectly ready to accept legitimate differences of view over when to take a specific action, especially when that action is as momentous as sending Americans into combat. What gets liberals into deep political difficulty is the perception that we are not simply opposed to specific uses of military force, but that we believe that America has, in principle, no right to act militarily except to defend our own territory.

Unfortunately, it is precisely this position that the

most vocal protestors of the war wanted Democrats to take. The biggest surprise I received in the postwar period was the series of angry meetings I had with activists on the left who were bitterly disappointed because I wouldn't extend my disagreement over the war to a denunciation of the lack of moral justification for America's position. At one point I was reminded of the power of the notsapostas for some when I told one meeting of peace advocates that I thought they should keep in mind that George Bush was morally far superior to Saddam Hussein, whatever the disagreements over politics. That set off a violent outburst from some of those present. In true notsaposta fashion, they did not deny what I had said, but, rather, vehemently criticized me for saying what they held to be both irrelevant and politically damaging.

The danger to liberals who voted against the war came not so much from a principled decision that sanctions should have been given more time, or that greater efforts needed to be made to share the allied burden. The political damage comes from an impression that we lacked sympathy with the rightness of America's cause. And this debate becomes a microcosm of the problem Democrats have faced in presidential elections, because it was exactly the most damaging political response that our left demanded of us. Voting against the war was of little consequence to those on the militant left if we did not give a properly scathing critique of American foreign policy to explain our position.

I believe my experience here illustrates the important difference between the way liberals can deal with this problem on the congressional level and the ways in which it causes us terrible difficulties in presidential politics.

I regretted that some of my constituents, most of whom supported me in previous elections, felt so let down by my refusal to join them in condemning American foreign policy so vigorously. During some of these meetings, and afterward, a few told me that they could no longer vote for me. But at these very meetings there were also people who agreed with my position, and others who disagreed with some of it but were nonetheless appreciative of the position I had taken.

The relevant political point is that at no time did I feel that the dissent I was confronting on my left threatened my political life. I have been in Congress long enough to have made clear the full range of my views, especially to those activists with whom I discussed the war. I knew that even among those disappointed with my partial support of the president on this matter my positions on other issues—abortion, reducing military spending, civil rights, housing—were still popular. And I was confident that over the twenty months between these angry sessions and the next congressional election there would be far more cases where my critics agreed with me than where they wouldn't. Thus, I felt no political pressure to move my position to the left to accomodate these arguments.

Little of what I have just said applies to presidential candidates. Rarely do they have the chance to become as well known as I am to those in my district. When a candidate is campaigning in presidential primaries, the election date is likely to be imminent; candidates have to be in many places and cannot spend much time in any one place before any one group of voters. Also, given the low turnout rates in primaries—and the even lower one in caucuses—articulate, ideologically committed activists have much more political weight than they do in the November elections.

For these reasons, and because it is a politician's nature to try to please the audience in front of them, the view of the ideological left has been more attractive to Democrats running for president than it has been to those in the House and Senate. During the nominating process those of us who disagree with the left's rejection of America's moral right to use force in the world must speak out more vigorously lest our candidates find themselves isolated on the left.

This does not mean that we need to support every use of force. Liberals have done so on several occasions in the eighties—contrary to the impression furthered by the right and the left that Democrats must always say no to combat. Liberals supported heavy military aid to Afghan rebels and the bombing of Libya in 1985. Both liberal and conservative opinion in Congress was mixed on sending American marines into Lebanon. The invasion of Grenada went ahead without Congress, but there was no general liberal objection to it after the fact.

Not all of these interventions have ended well—Lebanon was a tragedy in human terms and produced no useful result, and the outcome of Panama has been far less than promised. But our use of force to deter Libyan terrorism and to free the people of Grenada from vicious oppression succeeded very well, and liberals should acknowledge this no matter how angry it makes some of our activists. By doing so we win the right to make our case against excessive military spending on the Cold War scale, without having to defend ourselves against accusations that we are embarrassed about America's role in the world.

In fact, arguing against the current levels of U.S. military support for our wealthy European and Asian allies on factual grounds is a bit unfair because it involves countering arguments that are not really being made. George Bush doesn't claim that any tangible, military threat requires us to keep nearly 165,000 troops in Europe or to spend $5 billion per year on defending Japan. His argument is that we must spend as we always have because, as the leader of the world, it is our responsibility, and in our interest, to provide stability and to reassure other nations that we will be there to protect them against whatever threat may arise.

Summarizing an argument with which one vehemently disagrees is a difficult task, which I do not claim to have mastered. Obviously, those who want to understand the arguments of President Bush and his supporters against switching substantial resources from the military to the civilian sector should read and listen to what they say, not my version of it. But the Republican case does not even pretend to be accurate. The president and his supporters don't hint that they know of threats to the security of the United States and its allies that they cannot divulge for security reasons, or that we have underestimated the residual military strength of the Soviet Union, or the belligerence of the People's Republic of China. Instead, the president's position is that there is uncertainty in the world and that as long as there is, it is the responsibility of the United States as the world's leader to maintain a global military network strong enough to reassure others. For the past five years those of us pushing for military cuts to match the reduced threat from the Communist bloc have been told with regularity that we must keep up our very high levels of military might because it is necessary for us to reassure our allies. But I have never noted any great need on the part of those allies to reassure us. Nor have I been able to get the proponents of this view to advance any way in which we could reassure these allies for less than $100 billion per year of our money.

The basic flaw in the argument for massive American military expenditures to defend Western Europe and Japan on into the future is that the West Europeans and Japanese don't really believe there is a need for such expenditures themselves. They are happy to keep spending our money. But they are wholly unwilling—for perfectly good reasons—to spend very much of their own. In Japan there is, of course, a constitutional provision restricting their military spending. But no such provision keeps them from reimbursing us fully for what we spend on their defense. And the Europeans—and Australians, New Zealanders, and others—could increase their spending if they felt threatened. Instead, of course, they will all be reducing because the United States will defray part of the cost. Forty-five years ago these nations were poor and needed our charity—but not anymore.

In fact, a comparison of the rate of military spending in the United States with the rate of spending on weapons in this group of countries forms one of the strongest arguments for reducing American spending.

I disagree politically and intellectually with those who say America is in decline, the view that we have undertaken a global burden that we cannot fulfill. Analysts such as Joseph Nye do a good job of refuting that view. But this does not mean that there has been no strain on our society from forty-five years of defending the rest of the world. Even less does it mean that we should keep doing it. We can if we want to; but we shouldn't want to and we don't have to.

Rather than talk of the decline of America as a great power, the argument for the victory dividend focuses on the uniqueness of America's achievement in the Cold War period.

There have been two major competitions in the developed world since the end of World War II. Only the United States has been an all-out participant in both. On the one hand, we have been engaged in an all-out arms race with the Soviet Union. On the other, we have been engaged, especially during the past twenty-five years, in a vigorous competition for civilian markets with a wide range of nations in Europe and Asia. We have not done as well in either competition as we would have done had we not been so heavily engaged in the other; but we have nonetheless done extremely well in both: no other society in today's world could even have contemplated this kind of dual test.

The arms race has been a two-country show. It is true that other nations have acquired nuclear weapons, but on a spectrum of deliverable destructive capacity, even Great Britain, France, and China probably stood closer to the New York City Police Department than they did to the United States and the USSR.

What we now know of the grave political and economic weaknesses that have plagued the Soviet Union suggests strongly that we may have overestimated its war-making capacity, but it was nonetheless of super-power scale. How did the Soviets with their sick econ-omy stay in the same military ballpark as the United States? By using the only truly efficient part of their society—the mechanism of repression—to avoid deal-ing at all with civilian demand. The Soviets had a first-class military machine and a third-world quality of civilian life.

With our European and Asian allies the situation was close to the reverse. Japan, the star of the world in economic performance over the past twenty-five years, has benefited from having to spend little on its mili-tary. And the nations of Western Europe, while spend-ing higher percentages of their gross national product on the military than Japan, have still been able to aver-age less than half of what the United States spends. And since our GNP in the absolute greatly exceeds that of any other single nation, the total we have spent annually on our common military effort is orders of magnitude greater than that of any of our individual allies.

I disagree with those who argue that this burden is so great that the United States will inevitably collapse unless we set part of it aside. But it is equally wrong to ignore that for twenty years we alone have been in-volved in both the arms race and the civilian economic competition. Circumstances have forced the United States to try to be an international Bo Jackson, who amazed the country by successfully playing football in the fall and winter, and baseball in the spring and summer. The United States had in effect been playing major-league baseball and football against all-star baseball and football teams at the same time on the same field. Not even Bo at his best would know how to do that.

No doubt America would have done a lot better in one of these competitions had we used our resources overwhelmingly for the military, like the Soviet Union, or mostly for civilian goods, like Japan.

The Japanese have spent less than 1 percent of their GNP on military defense and very little on intelligence, while the U.S. percentage is on average more than six times as high. Obviously, this has had an effect on our ability to compete with them in the civilian area.

Take two of any businesses—retail establishments, service providers, manufacturers. Put them side by side with a municipal or state boundary dividing them. One pays more than six dollars out of every hundred dollars in revenue for basic police protection, and the other spends less than one dollar. The latter would have to have some serious problems not to be able to establish some real advantages over its competitor, in pricing, research and development, marketing, or some other critical area.

What this means is that in Japan nearly all intellectual, technical, and human resources go into producing goods for the world's consumer markets, while we have put a significant portion of our resources into making weapons for the common defense. It is here that liberals should be careful to avoid the trap of condemning America as a technological wasteland because we haven't kept up with some of our competitors in consumer electronics or computer chips. Not only do we continue to excel in other civilian areas, but we have been brilliantly successful in developing military technology that has not only served our international interests but has benefited our economy as well.

Whether one favored or opposed the war in Iraq, there is no denying the awesome effectiveness of our military hardware. American defense technology was both extremely well designed and proved marvelously suited to our war aims.

Suppose the scientists, technicians, planners, financial capital, and equipment that went into producing that weaponry had been available to produce consumer goods instead. If even half of these resources had been used by the United States in the civilian competition rather than the arms race, our international market share of high-technology products would be far higher than it is today.

And again, this is where the victory dividend comes in. There is no point, politically, in arguing about whether or not we could have benefited from a shift of resources from defense to civilian goods five years ago. What is important is for liberals to make the point—over the objection of the Republicans who insist on keeping spending high—that our society will now benefit from moving 3 to 4 percent of our gross national product from the military competition, where we have established indisputable supremacy, to the civilian competition, where we are doing well but could be doing better.

This does not require us to argue that military spending is a horrible blot on our society, or that there is no gain for the civilian sector in the technological advances that are made in the Pentagon. The point is a very simple one: resources are limited. The more we spend in money, personnel, and resources on defense, the less we will spend in other areas. And while indirect spin-offs can help, direct research in the relevant civilian fields would be far better.

This point is especially important for those critics of current American policy, both internal and external, who focus on the size of our budget deficit. No one has been more blatantly inconsistent than the Japanese and Germans in this regard. They simultaneously insist that we should drastically cut our budget deficit and complain loudly at any suggestion that the most socially constructive way for us to do this is to cut back on the massive amounts we have been spending for forty-five years keeping them free from Communist threats.

The position liberal Democrats should take into the 1992 presidential election is to propose that, beginning with the budget for fiscal 1992, the United States cut spending on national security in half by fiscal 1997.

(This lead time is necessary because so much defense spending is contracted years in advance, and because we have an obligation to be fair to the men and women who joined the military with expectations of certain careers. Fortunately, the military is an organization that requires large influxes of new people each year, making attrition a more effective way to make cuts here than in any other area of our economy.)

This means an end to a major U.S. troop presence in Western Europe. It means sticking with a nuclear deterrent of fixed-position land-based missiles, B-1 bombers with cruise missiles, and nuclear submarines, and eschewing the B-2, expensive MX or Midgetman mobile land missiles, and a massive Strategic Defense Initiative. It means providing Japan as much military protection as it wants to purchase from us. I do not advocate Japanese rearmament, but we can easily provide them what they need—as long as they pay for it.

And we can ask compensation from wealthy allies in other parts of the world as well. For example, in September 1991, the Senate of the Philippines asked American armed forces to leave that country. Why not ask our Asian allies, if they feel a need for it, to build and service a new base for our Asian operations? If they do not want to help pay for it, there is no reason for America to force it on them at our expense.

If liberals are successful in obtaining the cuts we want, we will confront the question of what to do with the new money. And this is where the victory dividend

is not only important in itself, but where it helps resolve another area of vulnerability for the Democrats—
the question of higher taxes.

As I noted in my discussion of the 1990 budget
fight, among the worst advice liberals get is that we
should show our courage and advocate higher taxes.
The fact that we can by 1997 shift approximately $150
billion from the military to the civilian sector of our
economy means that we can do to the advocates of tax
hikes in 1992 what Mondale should have done in
1984—disagree with them loudly and often.

Some part of these savings should go to deficit reduction, thus freeing up resources for the private sector. If we put one-third of the reduction here, we would
be $50 billion a year ahead of the schedule for deficit
reduction set out in the 1990 budget deal, and still have
$100 billion per year for necessary domestic programs.
We can then have the luxury of debating where to
spend our well-deserved windfall: repairing our infrastructure, building better housing, aiding education, or
any other areas that need attention.

And it is a debate where the Democrats' natural
advantages will come into full play. Virtually every one
of the programmatic uses to which this money can be
put has significant popular appeal, if the programs are
well structured. Even George Bush acknowledged the
desirability of increased activity in these areas in his
1989 inaugural. At that time he explained his reluctance to act on domestic issues, noting that our govern-

ment has "more will than wallet." Ironically, we now find him vigorously resisting adding cash to that wallet—cash that ought to result from American victory in the Cold War. This is a debate liberals should welcome.

Liberals can now talk of increased spending on domestic programs and a lower deficit without in any way jeopardizing the nation's security. We will have to concede to George Bush a greater sensitivity to the needs of our wealthy allies, and a greater focus on our paying the price of continuing to be the world's "leader."

But we definitely will not have to concede to him a greater degree of concern about important international issues. For we must state clearly that the victory dividend is not motivated by isolationism or a short-sighted focus on our short-term domestic interests. Some of the victims of America's excessive spending on national security over the recent decades have been important world concerns that don't have to do with arms. We have done too little recently about starvation and poverty in sub-Saharan Africa, or the crushing debt that undermines democracy in Latin America.

If we spend 5 percent of what we save on withdrawing our massive armed forces from NATO and asking the Japanese to pay fully for what we spend for their defense on programs to help economic development of the third world, we will be significantly increasing American activity in essential areas.

This means that when Democrats talk about taxes,

we can speak about making them fairer rather than about raising them. The debate that began in 1990 over who should pay what share of our overall tax bill is one that Democrats should be rekindling. Fairness is one of the issues that will greatly benefit liberals once we can refute the notion that it is a code word for tax increases.

The one area where liberals should be ready to support a tax increase is in the area of health insurance, and here we will be working only for a tax that will replace the heavy premiums most Americans pay for health insurance. Universal health insurance with a single payer financed by an equitable tax makes political and policy sense, and, like tax fairness, is an issue on which a mainstream liberal consensus is emerging.

With higher taxes off the agenda, domestic economic issues work heavily in our favor. Liberals can maximize our advantage here by making explicit our acceptance of the free-market framework, the left's notsaposta on this subject notwithstanding. Indeed, once we stress our understanding of the advantages of the market as a mechanism for ordering economic activity, we can convincingly argue that we better understand the economy than our conservative opponents. While regulation had a bad name in the early eighties, and can often be overzealous, the deregulatory excesses of the Reagan years have now become clear to the swing voters.

Our position should be that we agree with the conservatives that the market is a necessary condition for a prosperous America, but that unlike them we do not think that, completely left alone it suffices to provide a satisfactory quality of life for everyone.

I do not dwell on these domestic economic questions because I think our political strength here is clear. But there are two other domestic areas where we have suffered politically in the past—discrimination and crime. As in the area of defense-spending reductions, I believe that liberals need to pay more careful attention than we have in the past about how we approach them.

Crime Marches On

For the last twenty five years crime has helped Republicans in presidential races. Of all of the themes they have used to portray our party as out of touch with the values of average Americans, crime has been the toughest one for us to handle. What makes that fact even more frustrating is that the kinds of street crimes that most worry voters are exactly the types over which federal policies have the least influence. Yet in one of the crueler political paradoxes for liberals, this very fact compounds our political disadvantage, because Democrats have tended to respond to Republican charges that we are soft on crime by stressing how little the federal government can do to alleviate the problem in the short term. For many of the swing voters this only confirms the notion that the Republicans are seeking to get across: that we won't do anything to protect the safety and property of law-abiding citizens against the criminal element.

Crime is the most troubling problem for our presidential strategists for several reasons. First, it has staying power. Of all the issues George Bush used to discredit Michael Dukakis and erase the Democrats' lead in 1988, only crime has been a growth stock for Republicans. National security should become a Democratic issue. And when George Bush's lips on taxes turned out to be no more reliable than Milli Vanilli's, that issue also lost its potency. But crime marches on. In fact, the president used the crime bill in 1991 as one of his major points of attack on congressional Democrats.

Second, crime causes Democrats maximum political grief because it, more than any other area of public debate, is the place where liberals take unpopular views not just in symbolic terms, but on specific policy issues. Majorities of voters support the death penalty for certain types of crimes and oppose many procedural safeguards for accused criminals; they also oppose restrictions on the police. Liberal disagreement with majority opinion on how to combat crime has been overstated, in part, because ideological Democrats have made it acceptable for mainstream liberals to support some anticrime measures only as long as we remember we are notsaposta brag about it. Nevertheless, there are some undeniable conflicts between traditional liberal doctrine and popular positions on how to fight crime.

This point leads to the third reason that crime clouds the Democrats' political horizon. Because it is the area where liberal positions on some issues are least popular, it has the greatest potential for causing serious dissension within the party. In no other debate is the effort to combine Democratic positions with political reality as likely to mean that charges and countercharges of "sellout" and "fool" will rattle off the walls.

The reason for the passion is that crime has become—for conservatives and liberals—a marker for race. If America were a racially homogeneous country, the crime problem would not be a significant factor in presidential elections; states would write criminal laws and localities would enforce them, just as the Constitution provides. (There are federal constitutional rules imposed on this process by the Supreme Court, but few experts think these have had much of an impact on our crime-fighting capacity. In any case, a majority of the current Supreme Court is in the process of diminishing them.)

For most of this century, then, crime was not an issue in national elections, and certainly was not the problem for liberals it has since become. Neither Franklin Roosevelt, nor Harry Truman, nor John Kennedy, nor even Adlai Stevenson—hardly the em-

bodiment of law-and-order politics—were ever accused of being soft on crime. Then came the sixties, of
course, the period in which liberals became identified
with two attitudes for which they still suffer: having
too much sympathy for lawbreakers, and being unduly
hostile to the police.

Race is extraordinarily important here because it
was during the racial disturbances of the middle and
late sixties that the damaging perceptions about liberals began to take hold. And at the same time, the
growth of violent crime in the cities and active, vigorous civil disobedience by antiwar protesters helped ce-
ment the impression that liberals supported the dis-
turbers of the peace. The police response to these
actions became a major issue, especially after the Democratic convention in Chicago. A willingness to speak
out against police brutality and other misconduct then
became very important for those seeking support from
the increasingly organized and vocal left.

The unhappy consequence of all this was that just
as many Americans were becoming more frightened of
crime, more unhappy at disorder, and more supportive
of strong police action, they saw liberals explaining
away the actions of the lawless and harshly criticizing
the police. Most importantly, for many white Americans the fear of crime became a fear of crime by young
black males.

The first Republican efforts to take advantage of this
in the Nixon-Agnew law-and-order campaign in the

1970 congressional elections fell short. And by 1976 neither of these men were in a position to lecture on the sanctity of the law, so their party didn't push the question. But the respite was only temporary. As fear of violent crime became more and more a factor in American life, the notion that the Democrats were soft on crime took on more political strength. And the racial element of the crime question merged with the perception that Democrats were so much the prisoners of special interests that we wouldn't even support tough anticrime measures lest we offend some of these groups.

For many of the swing voters specifically, Democrats appear unwilling to stand up firmly against criminals because we fear alienating black voters. Of all the political misperceptions from which we liberals suffer, this is the worst—the least accurate, the most socially pernicious, and the most politically corrosive. It is also the one where all of our internal contradictions, guilt feelings, and disabling cultural lags work against an effective Democratic response. Unfortunately, especially for Michael Dukakis, these elements came together perfectly for the Republicans in 1988 in the person of Willie Horton.

On crime more than any other issue, those on the Democratic left must understand that the status quo is intolerable from both the electoral and policy standpoints. Continuing the orthodox liberal approach to crime will not only mean that liberals will be under a substantial political handicap. It makes it likelier than not that any federal crime policy will be mindlessly harsh and unproductively rigid. Further, it will maximize the extent to which negative attitudes on liberalism and race, which originate from the Democratic rhetoric on crime, will carry over and damage our position on other critical issues, such as civil rights enforcement and urban policy.

Race and crime together show the notsaposta syndrome at its worst. Liberals are notsaposta take note publicly of the statistical fact that young black males commit street crimes in a significantly higher proportion than any other major demographical group. We are notsaposta admit this because we fear that if we do, we will give aid and comfort to those who will draw wholly inaccurate, racist inferences about African-Americans and crime.

Yet when those of us who understand that the racial disproportion in street crime has to do with specific social and economic conditions and has absolutely nothing to do with any inherent racial characteristics become embarrassed by the subject, we leave a clear field to the vicious and ignorant who are prepared to race-bait. Whenever something is obvious and has a significant impact on people's lives, those who try to make believe it does not exist cede control of the debate to those who are willing to talk about it.

What happens, of course, is that liberal efforts to ignore the racial aspect of crime today rarely work, and when we do address the issue, we do so defensively and in a manner that exacerbates our political difficulty without effectively combating racism. Liberals over-argue the point that social and economic conditions are the cause of crime, and particularly of the disproportionate amount of crime committed by some minorities. By asking people to believe too much of this argument, we end up with their not believing as much of it as they should.

Of course, the point that social and economic conditions heavily influence the crime rate should be central to the liberal approach to this issue. And given the history of racism in this country, which begins with slavery, goes through legal segregation, and continues in lesser but still serious form today, African-Americans suffer most from these conditions and most often manifest their effects. But we must avoid the mistake of appearing to be justifying—or even mitigating—the actions of individual criminals by stressing the poverty and racism around them as if that made their actions less heinous. Poverty, racism, social disorganization—these all explain the prevalence of crime to some extent, but in no way do they justify it. We liberals have allowed ourselves to be restrained form saying what the public at large wants—and has every right—to hear: that people who assault, rape, rob from, or otherwise terrorize others are bad people from whom the innocent majority must be protected. Nothing in the contemporary political scene causes liberals more political harm than the perception that we are as sympathetic to criminals as we are to their victims. And we bring this on ourselves by telling each other not to speak too harshly of muggers and thieves lest we contribute to racism and an already excessively harsh penal code.

My disagreement with some of my friends on the ideological left on this issue is intellectual as well as political. I believe that some on the left allow their social sympathies to get in the way of their intellectual powers when they think about street crime. Assaulting or stealing from others is vicious behavior and society has an absolute obligation to protect the innocent against these thugs and then to punish them if protection fails. But my goal here is not so much to persuade those who disagree with this as it is to encourage those who do agree to feel freer about articulating it. For the fact is that out of a wholly admirable loathing of racism and a less admirable fear of offending our left, too many Democrats fail to say in public what they know to be both intellectually true and politically important: that society has the right to take strong action against antisocial individuals.

A related mistake liberals make is to use the bad social conditions that lead to crime as if it were an argument that will help persuade people to support social equity programs. In effect, we are telling voters who bitterly resent the incursions that crime has made on their lives that if we improve welfare benefits, fix up public housing, provide more job opportunities for minority teenagers, and do a better job of integrating our work force, the beneficiaries of this largesse will be less inclined to rob or beat them. This does not advance our chances of success.

What happens through this process is that a series of morally justified, sensible programs to improve social conditions comes to look like a form of sophisticated bribery. Measures to combat racism and reduce inequality have a far better chance of gaining popular support when they are defended on their inherent merits than when they are presented in a way that makes the swing voter see them as proffered rewards to get people to stop behavior that they should never have adopted in the first place.

The third major area of the crime debate where liberals must change our rhetoric has to do with law enforcement agencies, most particularly the police. There is no greater example of the way in which liberals have driven away our natural supporters than the recent political role of police officers.

For perfectly sensible reasons, public employees—fire fighters, teachers, sanitation workers, mental health specialists, social workers, etc.—have become strong supporters of the Democratic Party. At all levels of government, Democrats have supported a healthy and well-funded public sector while Republicans have been for shrinking the resources available for government services. Democrats are seen as friends of government and those who work for it. And all but police officers—and in some cases prison guards—tend to vote accordingly. This does not mean that all public employees who aren't cops vote Democratic. It means that public employees tend to vote more heavily Democratic than workers of similar social and economic characteristics who are employed in the private sector; these voters have become an increasingly important part of the Democratic coalition.

On substantive grounds the police should support us as well. Republican policies at the national level have been a significant cause of the revenue squeeze at the local level that has caused cutbacks in police departments just as it has in other local agencies. But police organizations are readily available for Republican campaign spots, and police officers are most prominent among those former Democrats who now vote regularly for Republican presidential nominees. This does not mean that police officers have become converts to the view that less is better when it comes to the resources available to them. The problem is that since the watershed political events of the mid-sixties, Democrats, to keep our left happy, have been pulled into a posture that police understandably regard as hostile to them.

There was good reason for much of the antipolice rhetoric and activity in the sixties and on into the seventies. Police forces in our big cities were overwhelmingly white institutions policing increasingly racially diverse communities. Policemen felt themselves under siege, challenged in every possible way by minority groups protesting their poverty and by young people rebelling against the war and the society that was waging it. And police force commanders were simply unprepared for leading their men into confrontations of this sort. The results were frequent instances of insensitivity, discrimination, unjustified force, and outright brutality. Police forces took on some of the characteristics of occupying armies rather than remaining indigenous, community-based protectors of life and property. This situation called for two sets of responses—but unfortunately it got three. The first priority was to make police forces genuinely integrated units with African-Americans and Hispanics present at all levels in reasonable numbers. The second priority was to institute procedures to lessen the likelihood of excessive force by police officers. This meant better training of the rank and file as well as of commanders, and also the use of new rules to stress the officers' obligation to do their jobs in a wholly lawful manner.

Fortunately, these two responses complemented each other. As police forces came more to represent the diversity of the communities they policed, brutality toward those communities became less likely. This is partly because police officers were less likely to be ignorant of or hostile to the people they worked among; and also because diversity meant the decline of a monolithic police culture that had fostered the us-against-them mentality that led to excessive force.

But the third response, which came from the left, was unjustified and unhelpful. It was the tendency by some to take the worst excesses of police behavior as the norm and to condemn law enforcement authorities in general as hostile by their very nature to those seeking political change from the left. This denunciation of the police in general rather than simply of police excesses was never as widespread among liberals as it appeared. I remember vividly the Saturday in April 1968 when, as an aide to then Mayor Kevin White of Boston, I arrived at City Hall to meet with leaders of the black community to discuss the disturbances that had followed the assassination of Martin Luther King. I was greeted outside by a picket line of white radicals who were demanding that all police be removed from the Roxbury area. As I talked with them, some of the black community leaders leaned out the second-floor window and pointedly suggested that I stop wasting my time with ideologues so I could come upstairs and discuss with them how the police could better serve their neighborhood. Minority group leaders—and those they represent—have always wanted better police in their communities, not the absence of any law enforcement.

This attack from the left on police in general— graphically symbolized by the labeling of police officers as pigs—was intellectually and politically flawed from the the outset. It is now an utter disaster on both counts, and while it has few adherents in its full-blown form, it still has a lingering effect on some liberals (and others, for whom one legacy of casual drug use in the sixties and seventies is a reflexive sense of the police as a threat). Antipolice rhetoric too often makes its way into our speeches; too rarely do we salute police officers for doing an extremely difficult job for too little compensation. And we are too grudging in our recognition of society's need for and interest in more effective protection against violent criminals.

In liberal circles it seems as if we are notsaposta notice one of our significant areas of success: through efforts begun in the sixties and over the objection of most conservatives, we have succeeded in making police forces better at both community relations and law enforcement. Liberal insistence on affirmative action—and in some cases quotas making up for past discrimination—has brought about the genuine integration of police forces in our cities, resulting in both more social equity and better policing. Similarly, lawsuits, legislative changes, and administrative efforts have considerably improved police rules and procedures. This does not mean that there is not still a problem with brutality, or that racial prejudice has gone away. Daryl Gates and the Los Angeles police are still realities, and not unique. But it does mean that liberals can take credit for improving the relations between police forces and inner-city populations and in substantially reducing police mistreatment of dissidents and demonstrators.

It means as well that, precisely because of this, liberals should approach today's police departments more sympathetically, without the traditional liberal reflex to find the police always in the wrong.

It is one thing for liberals to guard against the tendency of any bureaucracy to overdo its job. It is another to view an entire institution as flawed in its basic orientation, and to restrict its ability to perform its basic function. With the integration of the police departments and other changes that have been made both externally and internally in police governance, the time has come for liberals to state as clearly as possible that they support the police.

Because I think the police need all the help they can get to do their jobs, I differ with many of my liberal friends on the issue of police officers who commit procedural errors while making searches in good faith and for reasonable cause. Traditional liberal doctrine banishes all evidence obtained in this way from trials, lest we encourage police officers to rummage through our private possessions. I believe that the likelihood of random police misbehavior today has diminished to the point where it makes good public-policy sense to loosen this standard. Catching criminals is, after all, one of the best things government can do. Liberals must make sure that we are not confusing our objection to the fact that some kinds of private behavior are treated too harshly by the criminal law with our objection to the methods used to prevent crimes. Many of us react very angrily to illegal searches that result in people being sentenced to prison for smoking marijuana, or for possessing nude pictures. But most of that anger is generated by the fact that we are jailing people for such reasons, not that cops are trying to catch criminals. Were the same search conducted to obtain evidence against a mugger or kidnapper, I wouldn't mind the methods so much. Evidence which proves that someone has robbed, murdered, raped, or burglarized ought to be seen as a very welcome addition to the trial process. Unfortunately, for too many liberals, the attitudes carried over from the sixties won't let them recognize this fact. Indeed, some liberals continue to argue that there is some inherent virtue in making it difficult for society to win criminal convictions, even in the face of overwhelming evidence against a defendant. It is one thing to put up procedural fences that are intended to keep police officers from intruding on the rights of citizens. It is quite another to want to keep them high because of a generalized distrust of the honesty and decency of law enforcement officers.

This should be even easier for many liberals because the prime beneficiaries of better police protection are those at the bottom of the socioeconomic ladder. Fear of crime affects many Americans; but the actuality of crime is a terrible day-to-day reality mostly for poor residents of inner-city areas, most of whom, of course, are black and Hispanic. Liberals who join in fighting hard to get adequate funds to alleviate the problems that beset those who live in large public-housing projects must understand that protecting the law-abiding majority of those residents from the vicious criminals who terrorize them is a morally compelling thing to do. It is important for liberals to help to protect young black males against unfair harassment by the police. But it is also essential to provide all residents of inner cities with the sort of efficient, well-equipped police forces that can protect them against theft and violence. There is more of a trade-off here than some liberals have been willing to admit. In politics as in most of life, the more you guard against one set of evils, the less you may be able to prevent another. Focusing as obsessively as many on the left have on the historic shortcomings of the police has led too many to ignore the legitimate need for effective policing mechanisms. To the extent that the fight against racism in law enforcement continues to progress, I believe liberals should be willing explicitly to move the line in areas such as the exclusionary rule and preventive detention from where we insisted it be in the sixties to a position more attentive to society's interest in locking up violent criminals.

SOME LIBERALS have recognized the political problems with their positions on crime, but they haven't wanted to make the adjustments I've just advocated. So some have tried three alternative strategies that have proven politically ineffective. All three sets of proposals make public-policy sense on their own. But when they are put forward as substitutes for tough action against street criminals or for being more supportive of law enforcement agencies, the result is to make swing voters, in particular, suspicious of these measures without gaining any support for liberals on issues related to crime.

The first of these alternative tactics is the effort to stress how aggressively liberals pursue white-collar criminals. "You bet we're tough on crooks," this argument goes. "Just look at how hard we are on all those price fixers, inside traders, and executives who falsely label their juice bottles." This position has some political and moral appeal, and where those accused of looting savings and loan institutions or serious environmental polluters are involved, it can have strong impact with voters. But in no way is a tough stand against white-collar crime an acceptable substitute for locking up muggers or murderers. This becomes especially clear when some liberals make the terrible mistake of denouncing conservatives because they favor tougher sentences for those who hold up people at gunpoint than for those who play illegal games in the stock market. Most Americans feel the same way and for very good reason. I know very few people who, if asked to make a choice, would not prefer losing potential stock gains because of insider trading to waking up at 3 A.M. to find a hostile armed man in the bedroom.

Equally scarce are those who think it is worse to pay more for a household appliance because of monopolistic pricing than it would be to confront a couple of knife-wielding thugs in a dark parking lot. Liberals should be tough on white-collar crime, but they should not think that this toughness is in any way, shape, or form relevant to Democrats' political problems regarding street crime and how best to fight it. And they must understand that trying to pass off vigilance against stock swindlers as a substitute for locking up muggers worsens our problem. It further convinces the swing voters that liberals, as Ted Koppel said to Michael Dukakis, simply don't get it.

Gun control, another liberal response to crime, isn't the right answer either. Of course, sensible gun control is an issue which can have strong appeal to voters (although liberals have to be more sensitive than they have been to regional differences on gun restrictions). But presented as a substitute for harsher prison sentences or more prosecutorial freedom for law enforcement agencies, gun control will lose support among swing voters and will not help liberals to improve their image as crime fighters.

Indeed, for some swing voters, when liberals point to tougher restrictions on guns as a main part of our anticrime package, we are simply adding to the injury of taking away their guns the insult of calling them criminals while we do it. There are in this country a significant number of voters—mostly middle- and working-class white men—who enjoy owning and using guns for hunting, target shooting, and other wholly legitimate purposes. I believe there is a legitimate social purpose to be served in banning ownership of automatic weapons, in trying to keep firearms out of the hands of people with criminal records or a history of mental instability, and in keeping good records on those who own guns. And I vote accordingly. Few of these measures will do a great deal to protect innocent people against the sort of street crime that terrorizes them. But neither do they do any harm to legitimate gun owners, and if well enforced they will probably marginally reduce the level of violence in our society.

Liberals must remember, however, that the political costs of gun control are also high. There are a large number of people who care fiercely about what they believe to be their right to own guns without restrictions as long as they use them lawfully. And one of the major political problems liberals face today is a failure fully to understand what this means. These people will cast their votes primarily according to a candidate's position on gun control; they vote this way because of their commitment to the issue, not because of some clever manipulation by the National Rifle Association. The power of these voters is what makes even moderate gun-control measures so difficult to pass. It was resentment of Senator Kennedy's position on gun control that led large numbers of union members in Iowa and Maine to oppose him in the presidential caucuses of 1980 despite his leadership on virtually every other issue that mattered to them. The total focus on the issue of unrestricted gun ownership leads many voters to support Republicans for president despite pro-Democratic sentiments on economic and environmental issues. In many western states, for instance, it is the strength of these voters that leads liberal Democrats to vote against gun control, not some need for PAC money from the NRA.

This does not mean that liberals should abandon all support for gun control. But I do believe that an insufficient appreciation of the strength of these feelings leads many on the left to put far too much emphasis on this issue. Given the regional variations on the subject, when liberals insist on using gun control as a litmus test, they punish progressives in the Mountain states without in any way advancing the cause of gun control. The choice in most western states is not between liberals who favor gun control and liberals who oppose it; it is between a liberal who opposes gun control and a conservative.

At the presidential level the more fervently Democrats advocate gun control, the more we hurt ourselves with swing voters, especially in the western states. And by trying to make antigun laws serve as our example of how to be tough on crime, we end up losing ground on both issues.

The third area where liberal policy makes sense in

the abstract but not as part of a practical anticrime package deals with removing criminal sanctions against some acts and providing alternative punishments for others. To some liberals this approach solves the grave problems of overcrowded court dockets and prisons filled past capacity. The longer we have to wait to try those accused of crimes, the worse it is for society. Long-delayed trials are nice if you are guilty and hell if you are innocent, and swiftness of punishment itself seems to be of some real value as a deterrent. And even if a prosecutor gets convictions, there may be no place to incarcerate a criminal until after some other convict is turned loose. Thus, some liberals have reasonably proposed reducing violations punishable by imprisonment both to speed up trials and to make more room for those we are determined to put behind bars.

The trouble is that when liberals make these legitimate points without affirming the importance of catching, convicting, and locking up those who are guilty of street crimes, it comes across as one more example of liberal permissiveness. Too often this approach is presented as an indictment of society's vindictiveness. "If you weren't so hell-bent on putting people in jail unnecessarily," the liberal lecture goes, "you'd have less need for these nasty prisons." Usually, this argument is part of an assault on law enforcement for insisting on long sentences, and for being unwilling to grant parole more liberally. (Since 1988, even most of those on the left have understood the folly of talking too loudly about more furloughs.)

I agree with many of these arguments for reforming the criminal justice system. But the central problem here as in the previous two examples is that too many liberals seek to make this a substitute for being tough on street criminals. Our arguments for decriminalizing some acts and sentencing more flexibly for others will get a fair hearing only if we first establish our general toughness on those who violate the person and property of others.

There are two issues here—drugs and everything else. Liberals have argued against excessively harsh criminal sanctions for casual drug use and other behavior that often presents no real threat to others. But this is complicated by the fact that drug use is closely related to street crime, both because of the crimes committed by those seeking money to buy drugs and because of the lawless conditions in which drugs are bought and sold. It is complicated further by the greater toll illegal drug use has taken on minority communities, for all of the social and economic reasons that make minorities more vulnerable in our society.

Neither of these factors justifies many of the most rigid and unproductive aspects of current drug law. The absence of treatment for thousands of addicts who seek it; disruptive and intrusive random drug tests that serve no valid social purpose; ridiculously long prison sentences for first-time drug offenders; denial of government benefits to those who have used drugs; refusal of legal representation to those accused of drug involvement; and the waste of large sums on futile efforts to seal off the borders of a country as large and free as the United States. These are examples of grave errors in our drug policy and liberals should fight them wherever they can.

But as long as the general public sees us as predisposed to apologize for criminal behavior, our arguments will not have the impact they should and liberals will be dismissed as, once again, lobbying on behalf of the antisocial. Our ability to oppose ruining the life of a casual drug user and to protect a woman from being evicted from public housing because of her adult daughter's crack habit depends in substantial part on making clear that we favor swift and firm action against those who commit violent crimes against others.

Similarly, our opposition to imprisoning gamblers or to treating those who sell nude photos of others as criminals would appeal to people more if they are debated on their merits and not as part of an effort to justify liberal positions that question the need for incarceration and tough enforcement of the law.

Properly presented, the liberal position ought to be far more appealing to voters concerned about crime. It is we who support more revenues for more and better cops, fewer court delays, better prosecutors' offices, and more prisons. The limitations on taxing, borrowing, and spending that conservatives have pushed at various state levels rarely make exceptions for money spent to protect society against crime.

At the federal level the Democratic position throughout the eighties has been the one that would have put more money into the hands of city and state governments, the entities that have the responsibility for fighting the kinds of crime people worry about. Ronald Reagan and George Bush have done far more to protect Denmark and Belgium from attacks by Poland and Hungary than they have to protect elderly Americans from attacks by punks in their neighborhoods. But we have let them get away with winning through rhetoric what they should have forfeited by their actions.

Protecting people—especially the poor and racial minorities of the inner cities—is preeminently a responsibility of government. Nothing more clearly illustrates the political problem of liberals than our inability to understand and act on this central fact. And reversing ourselves is a key to a Democratic presidential victory.

The Democrats and Discrimination

Working out a sensible liberal position on crime is not only important in helping us to have a greater impact on crime policy and in improving our chances in presidential elections. It is also essential to winning acceptance for appropriate government policies dealing with discrimination. This set of issues is a prime example of how liberalism has created a political whole smaller than the sum of its parts; a series of policies that are politically appealing individually, taken together, have become a political negative in contemporary politics. And the most important cause of this is the perception that Democratic positions against racism, sexism, homophobia, and other forms of discrimination are taken out of fear of alienating special-interest groups whose agendas are hostile to the legitimate concerns of the majority—rather than as a reflection of honest convictions in favor of equal treatment.

For many of the swing voters the image of the Democrats as cravenly beholden to hostile special interests took root in the sixties and continues today in the image of Democrats as soft on criminals. This carries over in a decidedly negative way to the area of civil rights. Swing voters who believe that the Democrats back away from effective anticrime measures out of excessive concern for the sensitivities of African-Americans believe that similar lack of backbone corrupts our position on civil rights. This is why when George Bush denounces a Democratic-backed civil rights bill as a quota bill, all of the reality to the contrary avails us little in trying to refute the charge. What influences the decision in the minds of an unfortunately large number of white voters is not the specifics of the legislation, or the history of judicial interpretation of similar laws. It is the image of the Democrats as prisoners of the special interests—in this case black leaders seeking unearned privilege for their followers at the expense of the hardworking majority.

I am convinced that the positions Democrats are in fact taking on antidiscrimination questions are perfectly acceptable to the majority of voters when they are properly understood. And since many voters are the beneficiaries of sensible civil rights legislation, there is legitimate political advantage to be gained here. So if the unjustified negatives that surround antidiscrimination issues can be cleared away, a strong stand against all forms of discrimination would be a key part of a liberal Democratic platform that combines moral and electoral appeal.

There are four overlapping categories of discrimination currently at issue: race, sexual orientation, disability, and gender. (Religion was historically important, but America has progressed to the point where bigotry based on religion has lessened as a public-policy concern.)

These areas have some things in common, but also have differences in both their substance and their political impact. Analyzing both the differences and the similarities helps us understand the political factors involved.

The easiest one to deal with is the question of protecting people with handicaps. In 1989, legislation protecting the disabled passed Congress with broad bipartisan support and was immediately signed into law by President Bush. There are two interesting political points to be learned from this issue. There were some differences between the parties on this issue and they reflected greater Democratic support for the measure than Republican. During the amendment process it was mostly Democratic votes that preserved the bill against efforts by Republicans to weaken it. But the very fact that this bill received heavy Republican support both in the legislative and executive branches is more evidence for my general point about the popularity of liberal positions on issues.

What the Bush administration did here was to show its ability to co-opt liberalism when that makes political sense: a national statute mandating that commercial enterprises all over America accomodate themselves to people with various handicaps is hardly the stuff of traditional conservative doctrine.

Mall operators, restaurant owners, home builders, employers of all sorts—the list of private-sector interests put under strict legal obligations by this bill is as broad as our economy. It mandates that these private enterprises incur additional costs no matter what their customers prefer so as to ease the isolation and problems faced by people in wheelchairs and the blind. And it does so by a uniform national statute that overrides any state law that conflicts with it. Only one thing kept this legislation from being a major piece of contention between liberals who favor government intervention and conservatives who oppose restrictions on free enterprise: the wholly sympathetic nature of its beneficiaries. Because the groups being protected here—being given special treatment, actually—are people with whom the majority wholly sympathizes, far-reaching legislation that interferes with the economic decision making of millions of private entities was overwhelmingly supported. And in an exception that proves this rule, the only genuinely controversial aspect of the legislation dealt with protection for people with the HIV virus—the least popular category in the mix. While the principle of outlawing unfair discrimination ultimately won here as well, this was the one part of the bill that remained in question until the very end.

The Americans with Disabilities Act demonstrates the large degree of sympathy for those who have been afflicted with an illness or handicap. With equal force it shows how tenuous a hold traditional conservative doctrines have on the majority of voters, and how liberal notions of the obligation of society to intervene through government have become widely accepted in American politics.

That this far-reaching act was so uncontroversial is central to understanding the political debate over civil rights. For it demonstrates that what is controversial in this area is not so much the methods used to protect certain groups but the political appeal of the group in question. The more sympathetic the group, the less objection there will be to legislation that shelters its members from various forms of discrimination.

The recent legislative history of sex discrimination helps illustrate this point. In the debate over the civil rights bill in 1990 and 1991, opponents of the bill tended to stress race while supporters dwelt on sex discrimination. What both sides understand—but know they are notsaposta say—is that the same remedies for alleged discrimination are more acceptable to many voters when women are the victims than when African-Americans or Hispanics are involved. Politically, women do not not draw as much support as the physically handicapped when discrimination against them is at issue, but they do command large and growing majorities. When Ronald Reagan vetoed the Civil Rights Restoration Act, which had little to do with race and dealt mostly with the rights of women and handicapped people, his veto was overridden—unlike George Bush's of the Civil Rights Act of 1990, a bill about racial discrimination. Both laws involved efforts to reverse Supreme Court interpretations of civil rights statutes, and critics claimed that both bills went far beyond this purpose. The most politically relevant difference is that the first has to do with sex discrimination while the second was about race.

The popularity of defending women against discrimination has in fact been growing over the past few years as sentiment in our society has shifted more and more to the pro-choice position on abortion. At the start of this decade the political reality seemed to be that those who would outlaw abortions were in the majority. In Congress they were the ones who pushed for votes that could be used as bench marks in elections; everyone agreed that those eager to outlaw abortion had more political clout at the polls than those seeking to keep it legal. Whether these perceptions of political strength were ever true is arguable; what is not is that the pro-choice forces now have the political initiative. Today in Congress it is those who support legal abortions who are more likely to be seeking to have recorded votes on the subject; and they are far more likely to win when they are taken. At the presidential level, the pro-choice position has become a given among Democratic presidential candidates, while the traditionally anti-abortion Republicans have suddenly discovered the virtue of letting one hundred flowers bloom on this subject.

This matters tremendously in presidential politics since the desire of growing numbers of voters to maintain access to legal abortions is becoming a pro-Democratic factor at the presidential level. But it has also diminished the weight of the most controversial element in the drive to protect women against discrimination. For much of the eighties the abortion issue greatly complicated legislative efforts to outlaw sex discrimination in the broadest possible terms. Fear that it would lead to constitutionalizing the right to choose abortions is the reason the Equal Rights Amendment failed to receive the two-thirds majority that it needed to pass the House. The Civil Rights Restoration Act, ultimately enacted over Reagan's veto, lacked the votes even to pass Congress until its supporters agreed to language limiting its impact on the right to abortion.

Most important, the role of abortion in the early and mid-eighties was to detract from the overall force of women's rights as a proliberal issue. Now the reverse is true. Spurred by concern over a Supreme Court that seems on the verge of overturning *Roe* v. *Wade,* the pro-choice forces have gained strength to the point where the abortion component of the women's rights issue now adds to its political force rather than detracting from it. And Democratic identification with the rights of women to be treated fairly both in reproductive matters and more generally is likely to be a growing source of political strength for us in the nineties.

Now to the question of race: on this issue the answer to the Democrats' political problem with advocating strong civil rights protection for blacks and Hispanics will be found outside the specifics of the issue and not within it. As the examples of discrimination affecting women and disabled people show, the political resistance to the Democrats' civil rights stance is based far less on what we propose to do, and much more on whose behalf we propose to do it. So the solution is not to give up on the substance of civil rights legislation but to accompany our advocacy here by speaking out more forcefully against crime and for the rights of hardworking average Americans to keep what they earn.

Here more than anywhere else liberals suffer not because of the position we take but because of the voter perceptions that our values are wrong. This is the central truth in the argument that George Bush's use of the quota issue in 1990 and 1991 was a direct descendant of his use of Willie Horton in 1988. Of course, the two are not at all logically linked as issues. What joins them is the view of many swing voters that politicians who are so eager for black political support that they would allow a Willie Horton to be furloughed obviously have no problem in seeking to establish job preferences that disadvantage the white majority. This does not mean that the content of the civil rights bills is irrelevant. If our bills did in fact establish quotas, the Republicans wouldn't need Willie Horton to damage us politically. My point is that getting the legislation right—as I believe we have—is a necessary but not sufficient condition for winning the debate over it politically. Supporting the rights of racial minority groups to combat both explicit and subtle forms of discrimination will never be a basis on which liberals will win over large numbers of white votes. But neither does it have to be the political negative for liberals that it threatens to be today.

Once we make clear to the voters that we share their intense desire to punish those who assault or steal from others, that we value hard work and believe in a free-enterprise system that rewards hard work, and that we are striving as hard as we can for a society in which group identity will be irrelevant and individuals judged entirely on their merits, our support for specific legislation like the 1991 civil rights bill will have little political fallout for Democrats. We are suffering here because of what we have allowed people to think we stand for, not because of what we are in fact seeking to accomplish. What we must do in response is not to retreat on specifics—which would be morally wrenching for most of us—but rather work to put those specifics in a better, more politically appealing context. Fortunately, it is a context in which most of us do believe, and which we have refrained from affirming yet again because of a mistaken political focus on those to our left when our problem is with those in the center.

This brings me to homosexuality. (Textually. Since this is not an autobiography, I will not even try to speculate about what has brought me to it personally.) Had I written this book in 1981, this subject would not have appeared. In the seventies there were efforts to protect gay men and lesbians against discrimination at the state and local level in scattered places, but nothing of the sort had been seriously attempted nationally. On the contrary, until the early eighties the only votes taken in Congress on matters of sexual orientation involved successful efforts by demagogues and bigots to restrict homosexuals from participating in some government programs.

Had I written this five years ago—in 1986—I would have been confronted with something of a dilemma, given my commitment to the issue of combating anti-lesbian-and-gay discrimination and my eagerness to help liberal Democrats win the presidency. Most people would have argued that these goals were substantially inconsistent. By then, due to a combination of factors including the impatience of lesbians and gay men with second-class citizenship, the AIDS crisis, and some general societal changes, the issue of discrimination against people based on their sexual orientation was starting to register on the national political screen. And there were sharp differences between the two parties on the subject. In 1984 the Democratic platform contained language opposing discrimination against gay men and lesbians. The Republican platform ignored the subject. In Congress, while the antidiscrimination position lost as often as it won in floor votes, the Democrats supported such legislation by percentages more than twice as high as the Republicans. And on the Republican right there was clearly a readiness to make the Democrats pay a national political price for this advocacy of what most people thought would turn out to be one more unpopular liberal cause.

But it hasn't worked out that way. Several things have happened regarding homosexuality and national politics since 1986. Support for legislation strongly backed by lesbians and gay men has increased measurably in both parties, to the point where it is much likelier to win than to lose on the floor of the House or Senate, and also much likelier to be supported—or at least accepted—by the White House. While both parties have moved in this direction, the Democrats continue to be significantly more opposed to discrimination based on sexual orientation than Republicans. In the 1988 presidential platforms there was strong language from the Democrats on behalf of fairness for lesbians and gay men, while the Republicans were silent. In candidate questionnaires in 1988 all of the Democratic presidential contenders took generally supportive positions on lesbian and gay rights while all of the Republicans were negative.

In Congress from 1987 through 1990, according to the voting records compiled by the leading gay and lesbian organizations, Democrats have continued to support the antidiscriminatory position far more often than Republicans. For example, the voting tallies of the Human Rights Campaign Fund, the AIDS Action Council, and the National Gay and Lesbian Task Force show sixteen issues over this four-year period when a majority of House Democrats voted in support of the positions advocated by one of these three groups while a majority of House Republicans voted against them.

All of this was predictable in 1986. What was less predictable—certainly less predicted—is that this difference between the parties did not become a major drawback for the Democrats. Despite efforts by the far right to exploit what they assumed to be strong antihomosexual feeling in the country, this has not become a significant part of the Republicans' national attack on the Democrats' value structure.

While George Bush has used the racial issue against the Democrats in various forms, he has been publicly very silent on the question of homosexuality, and he has in fact enraged some of the true believers in his party by twice inviting representatives of gay and lesbian organizations to the White House for bill signings. Republicans in some states have used gay-baiting tactics against the Democratic presidential ticket, but this has simply not played the significant part in Republican national campaigns that other value questions have played. At congressional and local levels, there has been more effort by some conservatives to use this issue against liberals, but it has met with very little success. (In a few states, most notably Massachusetts, moderate Republicans have made major efforts to win gay and lesbian votes.)

By now there have been a large number of votes cast on issues of prime importance to the treatment of lesbians and gay men in our society and lists have been compiled by various interest groups that rate members of Congress on how they vote on these issues. These compilations appear to have had very little negative result on those who have voted to oppose discrimination against homosexuals. After more than two dozen votes in each house on controversial questions involving sexual orientation, I am not aware of any member of the House or Senate who was defeated for reelection in 1988 or 1990 because he or she voted to oppose anti-gay-and-lesbian activity. These facts are contrary to expectations many had in the mid-1980s.

There are several reasons for this chain of events. One of the most important is that, beginning in the mid-eighties, the most prominent congressional votes on gay and lesbian issues had to do with AIDS. Instead of voting on a controversial abstraction called gay rights, members of Congress were voting on public policies to deal with a deadly epidemic. As public-policy stakes go up, so does the willingness of many politicians to take risks. It is one thing to vote against a law decriminalizing sodomy when you are convinced that the law is never enforced and you are being asked to make a largely symbolic statement. It is quite another to vote against what you believe to be the appropriate public-health policies for combating a terrible epidemic. And throughout the period in which Congress has been voting on AIDS-related issues, the public health experts have been overwhelmingly on the same side of the question as the gay and lesbian organizations.

The fact that AIDS was the subject of most of the congressional votes relating to gays and lesbians in the mid-eighties had another effect as well. Large numbers

of gay men and lesbians who had previously been in-
different to or only mildly interested in national legislative action affecting homosexuality became highly
motivated. So just as the public-policy stakes were
being raised in this area, the force of pro-lesbian-and-
gay lobbying was increasing substantially. The result
was understandably far better for those fighting discrimination against gays.

Most relevant to this discussion, these develop-
ments turned out to be self-reenforcing. For as more
and more representatives and senators took the step of
voting in ways that opponents might describe deri-
sively as "pro-homosexual," they found that the consequences of doing so were not what they had feared.
I believe that many members of Congress first voted to
defy the right wing on gay-and-lesbian-related issues
reluctantly, feeling compelled to do so because life-
and-death issues were at stake, but worrying at the
same time that opponents would use these votes to
their disadvantage.

But as efforts to use pro-gay-and-lesbian votes
against the members who had cast them failed to work
in the elections of 1986 and thereafter, members lost
much of their political fear of this issue. Consequently,
today, even when AIDS is not the question, and Congress is voting instead on the sort of antidiscrimination
issues on which the antihomosexual side used to win
with regularity, the antidiscrimination forces are usually in the majority.

What has happened is that elected officials have discovered two important political facts: (1) there is more support for fair treatment for gay men and lesbians than many politicians believed in 1980 and (2) equally importantly, there is much less bigotry against homosexuals in our society than almost all politicians believed in 1980.

The first of these phenomena has been more frequently chronicled. During the eighties, gay men and lesbians organized themselves politically at the local and national level. This effort drew particular strength from the outrage and concern over society's response— or lack thereof—to AIDS. Helping this organizational drive were the increasing numbers of gay men and lesbians who were talking candidly about their sexual orientation to relatives, friends, coworkers, and in some cases casual acquaintances or perfect strangers. All of this activity meant that politicians—who are generally in very good touch with their districts—became much more aware than they had been not only of the presence of gay and lesbian constituents but of their concerns. It meant also that the friends, relatives, and others to whom people have come out offered a second layer of support. No organization has had more impact in its lobbying and educational work against antihomosexual policies than Parents and Friends of Lesbians and Gays. Few politicans want to argue with a father asserting his right to love his daughter as much as anyone else in America.

Less talked about but equally important, most politicians are finding that there is less prejudice in America based on sexual orientation than we had thought. The evidence I offer for this proposition comes from the conversations I have had with politicians who had opposed legislation harmful to gays nervously. They were convinced they were right on the merits, but they worried about the political storm. Members of Congress have suffered far less at the polls on this issue than they anticipated they would. This does not mean that no one lost votes; and obviously those most vulnerable to defeat if they alienated even a small number of anti-gay obsessives probably avoided the problem by voting against the anti-discrimination position. It does mean that there are many fewer voters prepared to make crusades against homosexuals a significant factor in their voting behavior than we had thought.

This, I think, is part of a larger social phenomenon in which race and sexual orientation are mirror opposites. Officially—legally and philosophically—America considers itself a nation opposed to racism. In fact, racism continues to be a serious problem in our society, and thus in our politics. The reverse is true with homosexuality. We have no national policies opposing discrimination against gays and lesbians. On the contrary, a presidential order banning gay men and lesbians from serving in the armed forces—a clear example of official bigotry—is still in effect. But as more and more gay men and lesbians make their sexual orientation clear, prejudice in our day-to-day lives, while still present, is diminishing. In short, I believe that America is both more racist and less homophobic in fact than it is in theory.

The major difference in my judgment is that the white majority feels far more threatened by nonwhites than the straight majority feels threatened by gay men and lesbians. People are far likelier to disapprove of homosexuality in the abstract than they are to disapprove of people being of a different race; but they are much more prone to fear racial minorities than to worry about harm coming to them from those who don't share their sexual orientation.

This conclusion has some significant consequences for liberals when thinking about how best to reestablish our acceptability to the national electorate.

Most importantly, this argument confirms the point that the liberals must become more credible as opponents of crime if we are to win the political battle over civil rights. And if we succeed in persuading the swing voters that we share the strong feelings they have on the crime issue, we need not retreat at all from the specifics of our positions against racial discrimination.

Also, the political realities of race and gender orientation make clear that integration rather than separatism is the best strategy for achieving policies that fight discrimination. Among activists in all three groups— feminists, African-Americans, and gay men and lesbians—there is a tension between those who focus on dismantling barriers to participation in mainstream American society and those eager to make radical changes in our society. This disagreement is ideological more than political. Most of those who push for wholesale change genuinely dislike significant aspects of American life and would pursue their agenda no matter what their race or sexual orientation.

To them political debate goes beyond specific issues to the merits of America's political and social life and the best ways to restructure it. They contend that, given the nature of American society, only a radical assault on mainstream values led by women, African-Americans, lesbians and gay men—or some combination of these overlapping categories—will have any effect. Most of these people claim that intregating their groups into American society is not only an unworthy moral goal but an unattainable political one. The discriminatory aspects of white, male mainstream American society are so deeply entrenched, they argue, that only a significant rearrangement of American social patterns can weaken them.

The question then becomes, which tactics have been most successful in fighting discrimination—those of confrontation or those of integration? Unlike the broad argument on the merits of American life, we can resolve this question empirically by looking at the histories of various antidiscrimination movements since the 1960s. To me the evidence is clear: the more a group assails the American mainstream in general, the more angrily it denounces its values and belittles its way of life, the less likely that group will succeed politically. This does not mean that extreme incivility in the short term will not produce results. The racial violence in the cities in the sixties may well have produced some short-term gains, and student dissenters frequently won concessions on specific points from university administrators and, less frequently, from local officials. But over the long term, all of us on the liberal side have paid a price for these gains in the loss of mainstream support for not only the specific movements involved but for those identified with them politically.

Not that civil disobedience, militancy, and unwillingness to compromise on some matters of deep principle are always politically unwise. But in my experience they are unwise when they are resorted to out of a sense of frustration and not out of a rational analysis of their potential political effect. I wish that today's activists in various movements understood better that Mohandas Gandhi and Martin Luther King were not only devoutly committed to the principles of fairness and equality but also very clever political actors who thought long, hard, and well about the impact their demonstrations might or might not have.

There is one enduring rule to be learned from this analysis: opposition to discrimination on the ground that, because of their suffering, victims have become more capable of showing those who aren't victims of discrimination how to lead a better moral life is about as counterproductive as political activity can get. Unfortunately, the tendency to make this argument is present among all of the groups discussed here, in varying degree; even more unfortunately, this attitude gets a sympathetic response from liberal political leaders. Nothing does more damage to the cause of antidiscrimination efforts than for liberal politicians to make our arguments for fairness part of an attack on the basic moral content of American society.

The consequence of indulging these arguments is to weaken us politically, particularly in national elections, without in any way strengthening the antidiscrimination cause. Indeed, precisely because this does weaken us politically, it leaves us less useful in the fight against whatever discrimination exists.

In summary, the best thing we can do to advance the fight against discrimination and to wage a successful national campaign on this issue is to make clear that we oppose bigotry as a sign of our commitment to American ideals, not as the forerunner of an all-out assault on how Americans live. Those of us who believe that America is good and just but capable of being better and fairer have a decided political advantage over those who view our society as a mean and selfish one in need of radical surgery. We err— and we lose elections—in sacrificing that advantage because we think the angriest people on our left insist that we do so.

Politics ain't beanbag, Mr. Dooley said, speaking scornfully of reformers. That's true, but it ain't football either—at least not in Vince Lombardi's sense that "winning isn't everything, it's the only thing."

Politics should be concerned with issues. People who seek the power to influence the lives of others through elected or appointed office ought to be doing so because they have a vision of how they can improve things; power sought for its own sake is unattractive, and those who are in politics solely to win elections don't deserve to.

But while winning isn't the only thing, to borrow Mr. Dooley's construction again, it ain't nothing either. It is hard to understand how people can profess to be seriously concerned about important public-policy goals when they minimize the importance of winning elections. People who do not win elections do not get to implement their ideas; their moral commitments then serve primarily to make them feel better, but not to advance the cause of those about whom they sincerely care.

Indeed, partly out of necessity, winning has come to be undervalued by some of my friends on the left. "There are worse things than losing elections," many of them argue. In one or two instances they are right. But from the standpoint of the liberal principles I care about, I cannot think of anything worse than losing election after election for the presidency—the office that is best able to implement them.

Theoretically, political activists can have significant influence on the electoral process—even if they never win elections—by using it to advance their ideas. But in fact, the result of the approach many of the most committed liberals have taken in the last twenty-five years has been exactly the opposite. I believe that the public-policy goals we care about have been retarded and not advanced by the mistakes that we've made.

It is precisely because we care about public policy outcomes that we are morally obligated to think hard about how to win. Adapting one's basic principles and the public-policy commitments that grow out of them to electoral reality is a complicated and uncertain business. On several of the most difficult issues for liberals, I have tried as hard as I can to advance a strategy that maximizes both our chances to win presidential elections and our ability to implement our public policy goals if we do. Of course there will be room for considerable debate about the choices I have made in trying to do this. But the issue that is not debatable is our need to make some hard choices. We cannot be certain that any particular approach to making liberalism more attractive to the voters is going to succeed. Anyone who has paid serious attention to American politics in the last twenty-five years must understand that we have to try.